To Fr. [illegible],

Happy Reading!

Best wishes,
Julia P.
Gelardi

DRINA & LILIBET

Queen Victoria and Queen Elizabeth II from
Birth to Accession

Julia P Gelardi

Cover Credit: (1) Description: *Queen Victoria*; Institution Collection-The Wallace Collection; Source-Web Gallery of Art; Date-1838; Author-Thomas Sully; https://commons.wikimedia.org/wiki/File:Thomas_Sully_-_Queen_Victoria_-_WGA21964.jpg. Permission-public domain. (2) Description: *Coronation Portrait of Queen Elizabeth II*; Institution Collection-The Royal Collection; Source-Royal Collection Object 404386; Date-c. 1953-1954; Author-Herbert James Gunn; https://commons.wikimedia.org/wiki/File:Queen_Elizabeth_II_Coronation_Portrait_Herbert_James_Gunn.jpg. Permission-public domain.

AUTHOR'S NOTE

This book is part of a series, "**ROYAL CAVALCADE**," designed to give the reader a glimpse into the world of Europe's royal families and the impact their lives had on history. I've chosen to show this by focusing on a particular aspect in the fascinating, moving, and often complicated personal and political lives of royalty.

Each book is for the general reader in that those with no prior knowledge of each topic can easily read the book without feeling the need to have had prior exposure to the topic. Specialist readers - those who have extensive knowledge of the subject - can also benefit from the book because the emphasis on a particular topic can lend new or extensive light on existing knowledge.

Thank you for purchasing this book, and if have enjoyed reading this book from my series, "**ROYAL CAVALCADE**," I'd be most grateful if you could post on Amazon a brief review and read, as well, other books from the series. Thanks again, and don't forget to visit my website at juliapgelardi.com.

Regnal Numbering:
Queen Victoria – the numbering of regnal monarchs in English history does not begin until there is a second monarch of the same name. That is why to this date, Queen Victoria (reigned 1837-1901) is not "Queen Victoria I." Victoria will be

designated as such when there is another regnal monarch who chooses to be called "Victoria" and that particular Victoria will become "Queen Victoria II."

Queen Elizabeth II – following the above explanation, Queen Elizabeth I (reigned 1558-1603) was known as "Queen Elizabeth" until Princess Elizabeth ascended the throne in 1952 and took the name of "Elizabeth" as her regnal name. Because she was the second of that name, she became "Queen Elizabeth II" and the other reigning monarch with "Elizabeth" as her regnal name became "Queen Elizabeth I."

'Heir Apparent' and 'Heiress Presumptive':

An 'heir-apparent' in a system of primogeniture is the person first in line to succeed to the throne. In a system that follows absolute primogeniture, a female who is first in line is regarded as 'heiress apparent.' In a system that does not follow absolute primogeniture but male-preferred primogeniture, such as what Princess Elizabeth (later Queen Elizabeth II) lived through, then the female heir is referred to as 'heiress presumptive' because it is assumed that her father is capable of fathering a son up to his time of death. Had Princess Elizabeth lived through a system of absolute primogeniture then she would have been 'heiress apparent.'

Simplified Genealogical Table

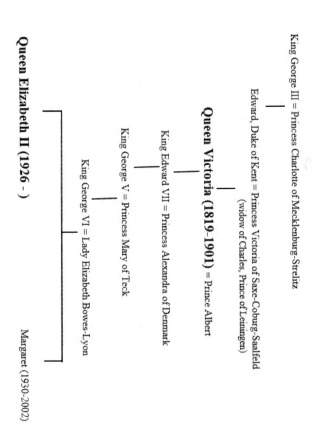

King George III = Princess Charlotte of Mecklenburg-Strelitz

Edward, Duke of Kent = Princess Victoria of Saxe-Coburg-Saalfeld
(widow of Charles, Prince of Leiningen)

Queen Victoria (1819-1901) = Prince Albert

King Edward VII = Princess Alexandra of Denmark

King George V = Princess Mary of Teck

King George VI = Lady Elizabeth Bowes-Lyon

Queen Elizabeth II (1926 -)

Margaret (1930-2002)

JULIA P. GELARDI

TABLE OF CONTENTS

INTRODUCTION

O n September 5, 2015, Queen Elizabeth II surpassed her great-great-grandmother, Queen Victoria, as the longest reigning monarch of the United Kingdom. Queen Victoria held the record as monarch for 63 years and 216 days. On February 6, 2017, Queen Elizabeth II became the first monarch in British history to reign for 65 years, thereby celebrating her Sapphire Jubilee.

The esteemed historian, Elizabeth Longford, in her biography of Queen Elizabeth II, wrote, "she is completely captivated by the image of her great-great grandmother Queen Victoria: her sense of duty, the care she bestowed on her dynasty, and the enormous power of her presence…" In many ways, Queen Elizabeth II has come to emulate Queen Victoria. Both have enjoyed tremendously long reigns, and both have earned the love and respect of their subjects. Their imprint upon history will likely last.

Just twenty-two years before the Queen Victoria's accession, Britain's Duke of Wellington headed a military coalition that defeated Napoleon at the Battle of Waterloo. When Queen Victoria ascended the throne as an eighteen-year-old in 1837, Britain was on its way to securing a leading role in the world as the kingdom powered through the Industrial Revolution. By the time Queen Victoria died in 1901, the Royal Navy ruled the waves and the British Empire had reached its zenith, with Britain holding sway over a quarter of the earth's landmass.

By the time Queen Victoria's great-great-granddaughter, Queen Elizabeth II ascended the throne in 1952 at the age of twenty-five, Britain had undergone profound changes. Though the United Kingdom was on the winning side of World War II, the nation was still recuperating from its hard-fought battles and the effects of the war. After the war, the British Empire began to diminish. India, the jewel in the crown, became independent in 1948; and unlike Victoria, Elizabeth II only signed herself "Elizabeth R," the "R" being "Regina," meaning 'Queen.' Victoria, on the other hand, had been Empress of India and had signed herself "Victoria R.I.," the "I" being "Imperatrix," meaning Empress.

The following pages highlight the lives of Victoria and Elizabeth from their births through their formative years, to their accessions. Both had, in their own ways, been destined for the throne; and when their reigns began, there was much hope for how these reigns would unfold.

The chapters in this book interchange between Victoria and Elizabeth. By writing about the two women in this manner, it is my hope that readers can come to have a new or better understanding of the fascinating early lives of these two famous queens.

Chapter 1. Victoria: 'Drina'

I n 1817, a crisis erupted in Britain over the line of succession when the Heiress Presumptive to the throne, Princess Charlotte, daughter of the Prince Regent, died in childbirth after being delivered of a stillborn son. The Princess's sudden death meant that that there was a dearth of legitimate heirs to succeed the mentally incapacitated King George III (Princess Charlotte's grandfather). A rush to the altar ensued when several sons of King George III sought brides to marry and beget legitimate children. In 1818, three of them married, including the King's fifth son, the fifty-one-year-old Prince Edward, Duke of Kent, who chose as his wife, Princess Victoire of Saxe-Coburg-Saalfeld, the thirty-one-year-old widow of the Prince of Leiningen. Upon marrying Victoire, the Duke of Kent also became the step-father of her two young children, Prince Carl and Princess Feodora of Leiningen,

Baron Christian Stockmar, physician and adviser of the Duchess's brother, Prince Leopold of

Saxe-Coburg-Saalfeld, noted at the time of the Duke
of Kent's marriage, that the Duke "was a tall, stately
man, of soldierlike bearing, already inclined to great
corpulency. In spite of the entire baldness of the
whole crown of his head, and his dyed hair, he might
still be considered a handsome man." Moreover, the
Duke's "manner in society was pleasant and easy,
intentionally courteous and engaging … and he was
not without ability and culture…" As for the new
Duchess, Stockmar noted that she "was of middle
height, rather large, but with a good figure, with fine
brown eyes and hair, fresh and youthful, naturally
cheerful and friendly, altogether most charming and
attractive."

After they married, the Duke and Duchess of
Kent lived abroad for a while to help economize, but
with the Duchess pregnant, the Duke was advised by
the radical member of Parliament, Joseph Hume, to
return to his native land. Hume wrote to the Duke,
telling him that: "The greatest and most important
duty your country looks for from you is for the
[German] Duchess to give birth on English soil."
Otherwise, the couple's desire to stay away from
England "will be thought by the nation to arise from
the wish of the Duchess to remain in her own
country." And so, the Duke and the heavily pregnant
Duchess of Kent set off from Amorbach in Germany

for England so that the Duchess's confinement could take place on English soil. In the very early morning May 24, 1819, a baby girl, "plump as a partridge," was born to Victoire, the Duchess of Kent at Kensington Palace in London. In a nearby room, members of the Privy Council gathered, for as custom dictated, they had to be present at the birth of a royal child. Not long after the Duchess of Kent gave birth, these Privy Councillors looked at the new Princess and declared themselves satisfied that a legitimate child had been born to the Duke and Duchess of Kent. The happy occasion was an event "which was destined to have an enormous influence on the English nation." The Duke of Kent was proud of his baby daughter, telling others that, "she will be Queen of England."

The baby's maternal grandmother, the Dowager Duchess of Coburg, was grateful for safe the arrival of her English granddaughters, noting that, "I cannot find words to express my delight … to God be praise and thanks eternally that everything went on smoothly … The English like Queens."

The infant was christened at Kensington Palace a month after her birth in an unpleasant atmosphere thick with disagreements and unpleasantries. A tussle over the names at the christening broke out when the baby's uncle, the

Prince Regent, did not want 'Charlotte' or 'Augusta' as one of her names. The Duke of Kent promoted 'Elizabeth,' but this, too, was rejected. Finally, the Prince Regent, in an acrimonious mood, glared at the teary-eyed Duchess of Kent, and insisted that the baby be named after her godfather, Tsar Alexander I of Russia, and hence the name "Alexandrina." As for the second name, the Prince Regent resolutely demanded, "let her be called after her mother." As he said this, he stared at the Duchess "whose elaborate curls and enormous hat shook with tempestuous sobs." And so, the baby was christened with the names, 'Alexandrina Victoria.' In her youth, the child was known as 'Drina' which soon was overtaken by the preferred 'Victoria.'

At the time of her birth, Victoria was fifth in line to throne, with King George III's eldest sons, the Prince Regent, and the Dukes of York, Clarence, and Kent, taking precedence. Drina, through her father, was a member of the Hanoverian royal family, a family that was notoriously dysfunctional and unstable. In fact, Princess Victoria "was born into a welter of family debt, virtually homeless, and was the object of mixed joy and anxiety. There was no proper monarch in the land, only an unstable Prince Regent, who was standing in for his father, George III. The king was still alive, but had become mad, and blind. The future succession of the Hanoverians was in grave doubt."

The Hanoverian royal family, with its faults and foibles may have been a cause for concern, but Great Britain itself suffered no such tarnish to its image. When Drina was born, Britain had entered a confident, glorious period. It was a century set to belong to Britain, one that began when Britain and its coalition partners defeated Napoleon at the Battle of Waterloo in 1815. It was also the beginning of *Pax Britannica*, with Britain on the cusp of becoming a major world power and empire. As the century unfolded, an imperial era would mark the century, a century that would be dominated by the reign of the royal child born in Kensington Palace in May 1819.

Drina joined a family that may have been illustrious but was marred by fractious relationships. Evidence of this friction was already in existence even before Princess Victoria could form any memories, for when she was but a few months old, her grandfather, King George III had threatened to take the baby away from the Duchess of Kent. The Duke of Kent allowed his unbalanced father to speak of it, but always tried to keep the King from exercising his will.

When Drina was only eight months old, the first great tragedy of her life took place when on January

23, 1820, when the Duke of Kent suddenly died of pneumonia, leaving a distraught, penniless widow and a baby. But just before dying, the Duke managed to sign a will in which he named the Duchess of Kent as the sole guardian of their daughter. Six days after Victoria lost her father, her grandfather, King George III, who had reigned since 1760 died. Upon King George's death, his eldest son, the Prince Regent, succeeded him as King George IV. Thus, within the space of a mere six days, Drina had jumped in the line of succession from fifth to third in line to the throne. After King George IV, there were now only Prince Frederick, the Duke of York and Prince William, the Duke of Clarence, ahead of Victoria in line for the throne.

The Duchess of Clarence, the former Princess Adelaide of Saxe-Meiningen, was a comfort to the newly widowed Duchess of Kent. Both women could converse in their native German and found in common a love and interest in the fatherless baby Princess Victoria. Adelaide was touched to see that when the little Princess was brought to her, "she held her two little hands over a miniature of the Duke of Kent hanging around her neck, and laughed as though delighted."

The Duchess of Clarence remained attached to her Kent niece and when Drina turned three, her loving Aunt Adelaide wrote to her:

> *Uncle William and Aunt Adelaide send their love to <u>dear little Victoria</u> with their best wishes on her birthday, and hope that she will now become <u>a very good Girl</u>, being now three years old ... Uncle William and Aunt Adelaide are very sorry to be absent on that day and not to see their dear, dear little Victoria, as they are sure she will be very good and obedient to dear Mamma on that day, and on many, many others.*

By the mid-1820s, the Duchess of Clarence remained childless and so too, were the Duke and Duchess of York and consequently it became increasingly evident as the years passed that Drina would inherit the throne one day. The importance of Princess Victoria within the British royal family was evident to John Conroy, an equerry to the Duke of Kent. Upon the Duke's death, the ambitious Irishman ensured his indispensability to the newly widowed Duchess by becoming her comptroller. Conroy thus became a permanent fixture at

Kensington Palace from Princess Victoria's earliest days, becoming almost a member of the family. The Duchess of Kent's reliance on John Conroy for advice and support was due in part to the fact that she did not enjoy cordial relations with her late husband's brothers. Not long after the Duke of Kent died, the Duchess declared that she and her daughter were "friendless and alone, in a country that was not her own." This reinforced the Duchess's desire to keep her daughter close to her. Another reason the Duchess chose to have Drina close by her side was that her brother, Leopold, who also happened to be the widower of the late Princess Charlotte, advised her to do so. Moreover, the widowed Duchess of Kent had little money at her disposal and still struggled with mastering English. She was tempted to return to Germany with baby Victoria. But this, Prince Leopold advised his sister not to do. It was essential, Leopold insisted, that little Victoria be raised in England and be fully English. This was a necessity should she ever become Queen of England. The Duchess of Kent understood her brother's dictum about raising a thoroughly English daughter who was surely destined for the British throne. Thus, heeding her Prince Leopold's advice, the Duchess of Kent consented to live in England with Victoria.

King George IV had reluctantly allowed his sister-in-law and niece to live in Kensington Palace in London, but the King offered no financial help to the Duchess of Kent. Instead, Prince Leopold again stepped in to help his sister with her expenses. It was thus to Kensington Palace that the Duchess of Kent, baby Drina, and the Duchess's other daughter, Princess Feodora of Leiningen, went to reside. Princess Feodora was twelve years older than Drina, but they grew close. The two sisters remained devoted to each other until Feodora left England to marry in 1828.

The Duchess of Kent was keen that the young Drina met some of the famous personages of the day. Invitees to Kensington Palace included the famed author, Sir Walter Scott and the abolitionist, William Wilberforce, who, to his delight, became a plaything during his visit in 1820, to the very young Victoria. The Duchess also tried to raise Victoria in an atmosphere that was not heavy with German influences. Moreover, the mother also ensured that Drina, who had no recollection of her father, would be taught to honor his memory and his service in the British Army. Victoria would, later in life, later claim that, "I was always told to consider myself a soldier's child."

Princess Victoria, of course, was no mere soldier's child, but third in line to the throne. Early on, the Duchess of Kent, aware of the illustrious future that awaited her daughter, took her role as mother of a possible future English monarch seriously. The Duchess wrote to a friend that when it came to her curious, happy, and willful baby, "I am already beginning to train her, which I am sure you will think wise!" That the future Queen of England was showing some stubbornness at an early age was evident when the Duchess of Kent wrote that at her baby at eight months old was "beginning to show symptoms of wanting to get her own little way."

The strong-willed baby grew into a chubby, pretty toddler with blue eyes and an animated manner about her. When she was very young, Drina followed a simple routine that involved breakfast with her mother consisting of simple fare such as milk, bread, and some fruit. This was followed by a carriage drive outside or a walk, followed by some instruction from the Duchess of Kent. Then came playtime, lunch, followed by some lessons, then time with her nurse, Mrs. Brock, and then dinner and bed. Since her earliest days, Victoria slept on a bed placed in her mother's room.

Among Victoria's earliest recollections was that of an old yellow carpet on which she crawled as a young toddler at Kensington Palace and of being frightened by some elderly bishops. The Princess's early life was dominated by her mother and Louise Lehzen. At the age of five, Drina's education took on more formality when Lehzen, a native of Hanover, became the Princess's governess. The daughter of a Lutheran pastor, Lehzen had already been a member of the Duchess of Kent's household since 1819. In appointing Lehzen as Victoria's governess, John Conroy and the Duchess of Kent both believed that Lehzen would easily follow their dictates and offer no opposition to their plans for Victoria. Lehzen would come to have a significant role in the future Queen Victoria's life. When Lehzen died in 1870, the Queen paid tribute to her, noting that: "She knew me from six months old, and from my fifth to my eighteenth year devoted all her care and energies to me with most wonderful abnegation of self, never even taking one day's holiday. I adored, though I was greatly in awe of her. She really seemed to have no thought but for me."

During Drina's early years, the Duchess of Kent might have gained some popularity if she had chosen to become more tactful and less jealous of rivals for her daughter's affections. But the Duchess harbored those jealousies and in so doing, chose to isolate her daughter from everyone but those the Duchess approved of. It would amount to a stifling childhood for Princess Victoria and one that was to be fraught with much conflict in the coming years.

Chapter 2. Elizabeth: A Treasured Daughter

In 1926, fifteen years had passed since the accession of Queen Victoria's grandson, King George V, to the British throne. The King, along with his wife, Queen Mary, had earned the respect of their subjects. As the parents of five children – four sons and a daughter – the succession was secure.

In the spring of 1926, London was the center of the British Empire, an empire so vast that it covered almost a quarter of the earth's land surface. It had also been just twenty-five years since the death of the venerable Queen Victoria. Queen Victoria's kingdom since her death had undergone significant changes. The Great War had inflicted severe casualties. Over 700,000 British soldiers were killed and wounded. Though only a decade had passed since the war, its searing memories were still raw. Nevertheless, British society was determined to enjoy life. Fashionable parties involving alcohol and raucous music in the capital were in full swing; and flappers, those modern young women with their bobbed hair and short skirts who enjoyed dancing, jazz music, and smoking in public, scandalized some and were cheered by others. To supporters of change, society was forging forward but for others, the changes were coming too fast for comfort.

Tensions between mine workers and mine owners were also high and reaching fever pitch. Owners wanted to increase the miners' working hours and reduce their wages. Not surprisingly, the miners objected vehemently. The British government was in the midst of trying to mediate between the two warring sides. In support of the beleaguered miners, the Trade Union Congress was threatening a general strike, one that was bound to have a devastating effect on the nation. Daily life would come to a screeching halt and "there would be no food in the stores, no police, no functioning banks, no newspapers, no public transport, but it might trigger a financial panic and an avalanche of crime. It might even, pessimists were predicting, bring on a social revolution."

It was in this atmosphere of taut tensions that Sir William Joynson-Hicks, the Home Secretary, hurriedly made his way through the damp and busy streets of London to the fashionable Mayfair district in the heart of London. His destination was 17 Bruton Street, the London home of the Earl and

Countess of Strathmore. For it was here that their twenty-five-year old daughter, the Duchess of York (née Lady Elizabeth Bowes-Lyon), was set to give birth. It was the tradition for a high-ranking member of the government in power to be present at the birth of a royal baby, and the arrival of this latest royal, proved no exception to this rule.

The Home Secretary was present at the birth of the third grandchild of King George V and Queen Mary, whose second son, Prince Albert ('Bertie'), the Duke of York, "worried about his wife and unborn child, fretted and chain-smoked and tried to smooth his nerves with drink." Not until his wife had been safely delivered by Cesarean section of a healthy baby, could the Duke breathe a sigh of relief. In the early morning of April 21, 1926, at 2:40 to be precise, a baby girl was born to the Duchess of York.

Ever since the former Lady Elizabeth Bowes-Lyon married Prince Albert in 1923 and became the Duchess of York, her life was lived in the limelight. Consequently, "her children were to belong half to her and half to the Empire the moment they were born. Her eldest daughter had to grow up and survive camera, cheers and adulation which might have destroyed her character."

When the Yorks' baby was born, the newborn's father wrote to his mother, Queen Mary, of his happiness at the arrival of the newest family member: "You don't know what a tremendous joy it is to Elizabeth & me to have our little girl. We always wanted a child to make our happiness complete, & now that it has at last happened, it seems so wonderful & strange."

That the Duke of York referred to his happiness being complete was no understatement. He had persevered in his pursuit of Lady Elizabeth Bowes-Lyon and finally won her hand in marriage. Once married to the shy, stammering Bertie, Elizabeth became his rock and source of support and strength. The 'smiling Duchess' as Elizabeth was known, had charmed many including the Duke's irascible father, the gruff King George V, paving the way for easier relations between father and son. One member of the royal family wrote of the Duchess in 1927: "She is perfectly enchanting and we all love her." This charm was evident in the Duchess of York even before she had married into the royal family. Elizabeth had been described by a friend as "being incapable of an ungracious word as she is of an ungraceful movement, and though she can express opinions very trenchantly and has a great love of argument, her manner is always gentle and disarming."

As for the Duke of York, he has been described by one who knew him, as one who had "a striving for the right course" and "though apt to be shy socially, if he finds an interesting and congenial companion he becomes agreeably alert, and can talk with great intelligence and acumen."

The first-born child of the Duke and Duchess of York was to inherit elements of her each of her parents' qualities, but such qualities were yet to be discovered when the Princess Elizabeth was still a baby. "Pink-skinned and fair-haired," the Princess was "an altogether neat and tidy baby, with shapely head and ears and long black lashes. The slate colour of her eyes quickly cleared to a light, bright blue." At five weeks old, she was christened in the private chapel of Buckingham Palace with the Archbishop of York presiding. Queen Mary's lady-in-waiting and confidante, the Countess of Airlie, attended the ceremony and recalled of the Princess: "She was a lovely baby although she cried so much all through the ceremony that immediately after it her old-fashioned nurse dosed her well from a bottle of dill water – to the surprise of the modern young mothers present, and the amusement of her uncle, the Prince of Wales." A biographer of Queen Elizabeth II noted of the incident that: "It was the last recorded incident of her surrendering to anything like a tantrum."

The baby, dressed in the same lace and silk christening gown worn by Queen Victoria's children, was given the names, Elizabeth Alexandra Mary, and was named after her mother; great-grandmother, Queen Alexandra; and grandmother, Queen Mary. Princess Elizabeth's godparents included members of the Strathmore and royal families, including Prince Arthur, the third son of Queen Victoria.

To the Duke of York, 'Elizabeth' was the ideal name to give his newborn daughter, for it honored his beloved wife. King George, a stickler for names, had to be convinced, however, that this was the right choice. Bertie told his father that there had been no daughter of that name in "your family" for a long time and that "Elizabeth of York" sounded especially nice. The King agreed that the name was indeed "pretty" and allowed the baby to be called, 'Elizabeth.' King George V also waived Queen Victoria's rule that all children in direct line of succession should carry her name or that of her husband, Prince Albert. "I hardly think that necessary," wrote King George to Queen Mary.

At Princess Elizabeth's birth, the baby – who was soon to be called 'Lilibet' - was third in line to the throne after her father and uncle, the Prince of Wales. The Prince was expected to find an appropriate wife in the near future and have a family, and so consequently, there was not much thought that the newborn child of the Yorks would easily ascend the throne of the United Kingdom. Two periodicals, however, did allude to the possibility. The *Daily Graphic* opined that: "The possibility that in the little stranger in Bruton Street there may be a future Queen of Great Britain (perhaps a second and resplendent Queen Elizabeth) is sufficiently intriguing; but let us not burden the bright hour of its arrival with speculation of its Royal destiny." Another periodical, *The Daily Sketch*, told its readers that: "A possible Queen of England was born yesterday at 17 Bruton-street Mayfair." The periodical reminded its readers that Queen Victoria had been the daughter of a fourth son of King George III and so, "it cannot be forgotten that our new Princess is a possible Queen-Empress." Whatever the future of the royal child, one thing was certain: "From the beginning, Princess Elizabeth was treated as a rather magical person by the public."

This 'magical person' may not have been born to be Queen of England, but hers was to be an unexpected inheritance so that by the time she was ten years old, it would become evident that she was just a heartbeat away from the throne.

Within a fortnight of Princess Elizabeth's birth, the General Strike broke out in Britain. Life as everyone knew it, was upended. "Upward of three million workers were out, including ambulance drivers and firefighters, hospital workers and the electricians who ran the power plants, and it looked as though before long the whole working population would be idle, bringing the entire country to a halt." The General Strike ended nine days later, but it had created havoc and stoked social tensions. Such, then, were the tumultuous days that followed the birth of Princess Elizabeth, who, of course, had no idea of the chaos and unease that surrounded her.

At home, the baby Princess was largely cared for by her mother's former nanny, Clara Cooper Knight, known as 'Alah' in the family, assisted by a young Scotswoman, Margaret MacDonald. It was under Alah's capable watch that Princess Elizabeth was left when the Duke and Duchess of York embarked on a six-month long tour of Australia and New Zealand. It was a daunting trip for the Duke who had to make public speeches despite his stammer. As for the Duchess, she hated being separated from her child, confiding in her diary that she felt "very miserable at leaving the baby. Went up & played with her & she was so sweet. Luckily she doesn't realize anything." And to Queen Mary, the Duchess wrote, "the baby was so sweet playing with the buttons on Bertie's uniform that it quite broke me up!" And during the return portion of the long trip, the Duchess wrote to her father-in-law, King George V, saying that, "I am looking forward more than I can say to the baby … I have missed her all day & every day, but am so grateful to you & Mama for having been so kind to her. It will be wonderful to see her again."

It was during this time of her parents' long absence that a special bond was forged between Princess Elizabeth and her paternal grandparents, King George V and Queen Mary, who, when in London, lived at Buckingham Palace. The baby, whom Queen Mary referred to as "a little darling," had also spent time with her maternal grandparents, paying visits to them in their Hertfordshire estate, St. Paul's Walden Bury. But of the two sets of grandparents, it was the King who seemed to have undergone a transformation of sorts when it came to his first granddaughter. A strict disciplinarian, King George had been a critical and difficult father but when it came to Princess Elizabeth of York, the King became a doting grandfather.

Baby Princess Elizabeth's ability to charm was not confined to King George and Queen Mary. The King and Queen's subjects had also fallen for the

Princess's charms, for Elizabeth's "brilliant blue gaze" had captured the attention of crowds of people who gathered whenever she was taken in her pram in one of London's parks; so much so that the Princess was "being mobbed by importunate admirers…"

In June 1927, the Duke and Duchess of York returned home to their baby who had grown since their departure. They appeared with Princess Elizabeth and King George and Queen Mary on the balcony of Buckingham Palace to greet the cheering crowds below. It would be the first of numerous appearances Elizabeth would make on the world's most famous balcony.

Home for the young Princess and her parents in London was 145 Piccadilly, a four-story white townhouse not far from Hyde Park Corner. It was a typical well-decorated home of an upper-class family that was run by a retinue of servants. Alah, of course, ran the nursery which stood out for its bright red carpet. Alah saw to it that the little York Princess would turn out to be a well-behaved child, as befitted a daughter of the royal house of Windsor, of whom the head was King George V.

In November 1928, King George V fell seriously ill with an abscessed lung. He went to stay in Bognor in the south of England to recuperate; and in order to cheer the grumbling patient, his favorite grandchild,

Princess Elizabeth, was sent to stay with him. The child's presence was like a ray of sunshine. Queen Mary noted in her diary, "G. delighted to see her." And as for the normally undemonstrative Queen Mary, she admitted that she played with her granddaughter, "in the garden making sandpies! The Archbishop of Canterbury came to see us & was so kind & so sympathetic." It made a stark contrast to Queen Victoria as a toddler, for her "earliest memories had been of a yellow carpet and terrifying bishops; those of her great-great-granddaughter may have been of a red carpet and a nice archbishop."

When he saw King George at Bognor, the Archbishop of Canterbury was met with a surprising sight: the old King on all fours, being led by his beard by Princess Elizabeth. Queen Mary's lady-in-waiting, the Countess of Airlie, was taken aback by the transformation in the King, for she had never seen him play with his own children when they were young. The Countess of Airlie saw how King George favored Princess Elizabeth who "always came first in his affections" and that "his convalescence at Bognor was bearable to him" thanks to his granddaughter's presence. The residents of Bognor were treated to a charming portrait of the recuperating King George and his little granddaughter on their walks; the King in his bath chair, Elizabeth toddling along next to him. Those who watched them could hear the King's voice which "boomed like the sea under the March winds; hers was high and clear as his little golden hand-bell at Buckingham Palace."

Princess Elizabeth was fortunate in that not only did she have doting grandparents, but parents as well who wanted for their daughter, a happy childhood. For the Duke of York "never forgot the miseries of a frustrated childhood." And "for the opposite reasons the Duchess had exactly the same dream" for whatever children would be born to her. "A rapturous and serene childhood" that had been denied the Duke but enjoyed by the Duchess would be had for Elizabeth and any future sibling.

.

Chapter 3. Victoria: The Kensington System

Drina's childhood home, Kensington Palace, was at the time of her formative years, a quiet oasis in comparison to other, more hectic parts of London. The palace was also home to the Princess's uncle, the Duke of Sussex, another of King George III's sons, and of Sussex's sister, Princess Sophia. Their brother, King George IV, had never been fond of the Duchess of Kent, and had only grudgingly allowed her to live at Kensington.

Drina had few playmates as she grew up; Princess Feodora was one of them as was Victoire Conroy, a daughter of John Conroy, though Victoire never became a friend of Drina's. Consequently, the lack of companions her age meant that the young Princess formed an attachment to her collection of numerous dolls, numbering over 130.

As the years came and went, playtime made way for more formal lessons. Louise Lehzen was joined by the Reverend George Davys to oversee Princess

Victoria's education. Besides religion, arithmetic, and history, Drina was taught penmanship and languages. She acquired a fluency in German and French and liked learning Italian. The Princess was not keen on literature but much enjoyed music and art. She eventually became an accomplished artist, her forte being drawing and painting in watercolors.

As the Princess was a willful child, efforts to curb her stubbornness and instill good character and manners were part of the education process. Lehzen's goal was to mold the Princess into a self-disciplined, honest, and well-mannered girl. She had Victoria write into 'Behaviour Books,' her self-assessment of her actions. The young Princess did not mince words in various entries. In 1832, she recorded that she was, "VERY VERY VERY VERY HORRIBLY NAUGHTY!!!!" And once, when a tutor asked the Duchess of Kent if Princess Victoria had been good, the Duchess said yes she had but there had been a little storm, to which Victoria chimed in: "Two storms – one at dressing and one at washing." And once, when Victoria had to endure piano lessons, and was told that she must practice, the annoyed child shut the piano with a loud bang and declared: "There! You see there is no *must* about it."

Raising a future Queen of England had its challenges. Drina acquired early on, a sense of exalted status that had to be curbed. The Princess once told a child who was about to play with some of her toys: "You must not touch those, they are mine: and I may call you Jane, but you must not call me Victoria."

Princess Victoria did not suffer from shyness but did exhibit a sensitive and artistic nature. She especially liked attending the ballet, opera, and the theater and this interest was reflected in the way she dressed her dolls. They had costumes based on the stars of the shows Victoria attended. To the young Victoria, her world largely revolved around her dolls, her mother, Lehzen, and life at Kensington Palace, but already she was being seen as an important personage in the land as evidenced by the granting of an official allowance by the British Parliament to the Duchess of Kent in 1825. Princess Victoria's importance continued to be in the ascendant. In 1827, When the Princess was seven, her uncle, the Duke of York died which meant that only the Duke of Clarence was ahead of the Princess in the line of succession, thus increasing Victoria's importance as a member of the British royal family.

As the Princess's importance increased, John Conroy's ambitions grew in tandem. He managed to get King George IV, as King of Hanover, to create him a Knight Commander of the Hanoverian Order. As such, he was now 'Sir John Conroy.' Conroy expected that as his influence over young Drina and her mother increased, he would eventually be rewarded with Victoria's loyalty and gratitude after her accession to the throne. In explaining his plans for Princess Victoria, Conroy told her half-brother, the Prince of Leiningen, of his laudable aim that the Princess was to be given "an upbringing which would enable her in the future to be equal to her high position." Moreover, Conroy intended "to win her so high a place in the hearts of her future subjects, even before her accession that she would assume the scepter with a popularity never yet attained and rule with *commensurate* power." As for the Duchess of Kent, "every effort must be made to keep the education of the daughter completely in the hands of her mother and to prevent all interference … *nothing* and *no one* should be able to tear the daughter away from her." This words by Conroy encapsulate what became known as the 'Kensington System' which was used in the serious endeavor of educating and molding Princess Victoria.

Sadly for the Princess, Sir John Conroy's influence upon the Duchess of Kent was virtually complete. He was her comptroller and adviser and entrenched himself at the Duchess's side, portraying himself as someone who had her full interests, and her daughter's to heart. As for Louise Lehzen, Conroy saw her as no threat, and so had no objections to having her employed in Kensington Palace. By having her created a Hanoverian Baroness by King George IV, Conroy ensured that Lehzen was not seen as too lowly a retainer to be in charge of the care of Princess Victoria.

The Kensington System soon became oppressive for Drina. She was treated somewhere in between that of being something of a precious jewel that could not be lost, to an invalid who could not think for herself and had to be protected from herself and others. Consequently, Drina was never left alone. She continued to sleep in her mother's bedroom on a bed placed near her mother's. Baroness Lehzen sat with the Princess in the bedroom until the Duchess arrived to retire for the evening. Victoria could not walk down the stairs unless someone was holding her hand, nor could she see anyone unless another person was present. But it was not only the physical well-being of Drina that drove the Kensington System. "Above all, the system was devised to keep Victoria as far as possible isolated from the decadent English Hanoverian court, and the almost equally dissipated and extravagant Coburg court..." But because Princess Victoria lived in proximity not to her Coburg, but to her Hanoverian relations, it was her isolation from this family that was of the utmost importance.

The success of the Kensington System stemmed in large part from the successful isolation of Princess Victoria from any outside influence that might interfere with the Duchess of Kent and Conroy's plans. This meant that the Princess had to be kept away as much as possible from the British royals. The nation needed to see that unlike her late father's family, Princess Victoria was being raised in a higher moral standard, very "different ... from those of the English Royal family, against whom so many public accusations of misconduct persisted." This was not difficult on the Duchess's part since her relations with the royals continued to be strained. And yet the Duchess knew there were certain occasions when it was necessary to bring her daughter to court. Such was the case in 1826 when King George IV, who, though he continued to dislike his sister-in-law, nevertheless understood the growing importance of Princess Victoria and invited her and her mother to visit him. Princess Victoria's obese and extravagant 'Uncle King' was charmed by his young niece with the large blue eyes, brown curls, and trusting disposition. The King affectionately asked her to, "give me you little paw," and Victoria willingly clasped her uncle's hand. In another visit of Victoria's in 1829, King George had declared that he delighted in "her charming 'manners."

In writing about this visit, Victoria's maternal grandmother at Coburg wrote to her daughter, the Duchess of Kent, about the Princess: "The little monkey must have pleased and amused him [the King], she is such a pretty, clever child."

Another individual, Mrs. Arbuthnot, who met the Princess in 1828, had expressed similar observations about Victoria, declaring that she "is the most charming child I ever saw. She is a fine, beautifully made, handsome creature, quite playful & childish playing with her dolls and in high spirits, but civil and well bread & Princess like to the greatest degree." The mother, in Mrs. Arbuthnot's eyes, had done well: "The Duchess of Kent is a very sensible person and educates her remarkably well."

In June 1830, King George IV died and was succeeded by his brother, the Duke of Clarence, who became King William IV, at the age of sixty-four. A gruff sailor, whose "oaths of the hottest sort flew from his lips, like sparks from an anvil," William IV had many flaws. As one chronicler put it, "at no time was he remarkable for his intellect, tractability, or social manners." Such was the man who was the uncle of Princess Victoria and the husband of Queen Adelaide.

Queen Adelaide continued to remain childless (losing a four-month-old daughter in 1820 and giving birth to stillborn twin sons in 1822) and yet she never came to resent Princess Victoria. On the contrary, Adelaide continued to be fond of her niece and did not begrudge her for being the next in line to the throne. When King William first opened Parliament, the Queen watched the procession, accompanied by Princess Victoria. When the crowd cried, 'The Queen!' to Adelaide, she carried little Drina in her arms, which electrified the crowds who then cheered, "God Save both Queens!"

A measure of how Queen Adelaide felt about her niece came in a note she wrote the Duchess of Kent, telling her in poignant terms that: "My children are dead, but yours lives, and she is mine too."

At the end of 1830, the question of a regency for Princess Victoria in the event of King William's death was settled when it was decided that the Duchess of Kent would become regent. The possibility that she may be regent before Victoria attained her eighteenth birthday, whereby she could reign on her own, raised the status of the Duchess and pleased her and Sir John Conroy immensely.

Conroy immediately set about composing a memorandum "defining the powers which could be exercised by the Sovereign over the heir presumptive to the throne." As one historian has noted, "attempts at interferences by King William IV were expected and the Duchess of Kent and Conroy wished to be prepared in their legal rights."

With her position as regent secure, the Duchess of Kent began to isolate her daughter from King William and Queen Adelaide – a move which embittered the King and saddened the Queen, for both had genuinely loved their niece. The Duchess, however, was adamant. Not only was she "extremely jealous of any divided authority," the Duchess was also "determined that her daughter should be guided by her influence in everything." The main excuse used by the Duchess to keep Drina away from King William's court was the fact that the child might come into contact with the King's ten illegitimate children, the FitzClarences. The King and Queen kept on close terms with the FitzClarences and welcomed them at court.

The Duchess of Kent had been successful in keeping her daughter from the King's court, but in 1831, Drina attended her first drawing-room audience held by Queen Adelaide. It was hoped that the Princess would be present at the coronation of

King William and Queen Adelaide, but when the Duchess of Kent saw that her daughter's precedence at the ceremony was not to her liking, the Duchess resolutely refused to attend the coronation and barred Drina from attending it as well. Upon learning that Princess Victoria would not precede the King's younger brothers in precedence but follow them instead, the Duchess of Kent objected. The Duchess insisted that her daughter, as Heiress Presumptive, must be ahead of her uncles in the royal procession. The excuse the Duchess of Kent gave for her and her daughter's absence from the event was the Princess's delicate health. *The Times* objected to the Duchess of Kent's refusal to attend the coronation and her refusal to allow Princess Victoria to attend as well. The newspaper, in an editorial, explained to its readers that, "the Duchess of Kent is grossly mistaken if she thinks to ingratiate herself with the people of this country by opposition to the will and disrespect to the power of the King." Drina's absence from King William IV's coronation greatly upset the twelve-year-old Princess who shed tears over the incident. "Nothing could console me," she later recalled, "not even my dolls."

Princess Victoria continued to grow up in a hothouse atmosphere of conflict. The previously close, sister-like relationship between the Duchess of

Kent and Queen Adelaide had by now been broken. When Belgium became independent from the Netherlands in 1830, the Duchess's brother, Leopold was chosen as Belgium's new monarch. Naturally, the Duchess supported her brother who had become Belgium's King Leopold I. Queen Adelaide opposed Belgium's independence, and so the two sisters-in-law saw their close relationship disintegrate, to the detriment of Princess Victoria. Moreover, the Duchess's desire to be made Dowager Princess of Wales by virtue of her position as mother of the heiress to the throne, was rejected. She was also denied the control of the allowance owed to her and Drina. All this amounted in the Duchess of Kent's mind, to evidence that she was surrounded by enemies. And this, in turn, meant that the Duchess would jealously guard her daughter and ensure that her formative years would be spent at Kensington Palace – a place that was to be not just her home, also her gilded prison.

Sir John Conroy, who carefully cultivated useful friendships, such as those of Drina's aunt, Princess Sophia, and uncle, the Duke of Sussex, curiously never chose to cultivate and charm the one person who was the key to his power and prestige – Princess Victoria. On the contrary, Conroy wanted to make sure that the Princess saw herself as subordinate to her mother and to him at all times. This, Princess Victoria, grew to resent. And as she saw her mother fall increasingly under Sir John Conroy's influence, the daughter saw in her devoted Lehzen, a trustful refuge.

And so, as Baroness Lehzen continued to guide her charge and offer her security, Lehzen also grew wise in that she avoided the resentments, intrigues, and discord that swirled about Kensington Palace. Lehzen saw how the Baroness Späth, who had been with the Duchess of Kent for many years, was summarily dismissed when she spoke out of turn to the Duchess. Rumors swirled that the Duchess and Conroy were romantically linked, but this the Duchess ignored and continued to keep Conroy by her side. Eventually, the Duchess and Conroy realized that Lehzen was not the compliant, malleable creature they assumed her to be, but by that time, when Princess Victoria was about ten, Lehzen, could not be dislodged from Kensington Palace. She had proven to be a diligent governess who had influence over the strong-willed Princess.

Life at Kensington Palace for Princess Victoria under the Kensington System was a suffocating one, one that was not to abate as the Princess's station in life continued to rise. Because this was so, Sir John Conroy tried to ensure that his tyrannical hold over the Princess and her mother would continue to grow.

Chapter 4. Elizabeth: "Lilibet"

When Princess Elizabeth had been born, the Duke of York assured his father that there would be no confusion in the fact that his daughter and wife would be sharing the same names, and he was right. Not long after the Princess began to talk, she was challenged by the pronunciation of her name. She could not master 'Elizabeth' but instead said, 'Lilibet,' and it was as Lilibet that she became known to her family and friends.

When Lady Cynthia Asquith met the very young Princess who was then just learning to take her first steps, Lady Cynthia noted that Elizabeth liked to refer to herself in the third person. The little Princess entranced Lady Cynthia by saying such charming phrases as: "Lilibet walk Self" or "Lilibet thut door Self." Lady Cynthia thought Lilibet to be an engaging girl, and "already had that mysterious quality called personality – a quality as undefinable as unmistakable." Lilibet entered a room with "very definite dignity, she was graciously pleased to be amiable." Lilibet also exhibited a quick awareness of the world around her as she meticulously went through Lady Cynthia's things. "She deftly relieved me of my handbag," recalled the visitor, "and displayed a precocious sense of the proper use of all its contents. Spectacles were at once perched on to the tiny nose, pennies pocketed, the mirror ogled and face-powder deftly applied." At five years of age, Princess Elizabeth again impressed Lady Cynthia with her precociousness, noting that, "she did the honours of her nursery with the manners of an ambassadress, offering me food with the unpressing politeness of a perfect hostess, and showing herself a good listener as well as a good conversationalist." Lady Cynthia was left with the impression of Princess Elizabeth that, "in spite of the correctness of her behaviour, she was full of spirits as ever, and I remember thinking that I had never met any child who seemed more in love with life."

Clearly the Duke and Duchess of York and Alah were doing a fine job in raising little Princess Elizabeth. That the domestic life of the Yorks was a joyous one was alluded to by none other than Princess Elizabeth's mother, who once asked: "Why should anybody want to hear about our home life?" After all, "it is just like that of any other happy home."

This happy home life was augmented with the arrival in 1930 of a new member: a daughter, born in August at Glamis Castle, the Scottish home of the baby's maternal grandparents, the Earl and Countess of Strathmore. In announcing the arrival of her new sister to a visitor, Princess Elizabeth said, "I've got a Baby Sister – Margaret Rose – and I'm going to call her Bud!"

"Why Bud?"

"Well, she's not a real rose, is she yet? She's only a bud."

The arrival of Princess Margaret Rose did not faze Princess Elizabeth, nor did it elicit feelings of jealousy in her. She welcomed her baby sister and continued to be a good and dutiful child. By this time, Princess Elizabeth's personality could be easily discerned. She was not only clever and proper, she also, in her father's eyes, had inherited "her great-great-grandmother Queen Victoria's pronounced individuality, if not her stern demeanor." Lilibet, like Victoria, had a "clear ringing voice" and the same "decided manner, a bright-faced intelligence, and strong opinions."

Princess Elizabeth's popularity, coupled with that of her parents, continued to grow even with the arrival of Princess Margaret Rose. Presents were sent to Elizabeth from all over the Empire and her face was well-known. Her young face graced stamps; in 1933, Newfoundland issued a stamp with her portrait based on a photograph by the British society photographer, Marcus Adams. The image presented by the Duke and Duchess of York with their two photogenic children contributed much to people's view of them as the epitome of domestic bliss, which, in turn, helped to bolster the image of the British monarchy.

The happiness experienced within the York household could not be found among other members of the royal family. Princess Elizabeth in her early years was unaware of the friction and unease that marked the relations between her grandfather and his sons, especially when it came to the King and his heir, the Prince of Wales, known in the family as 'David.' David had become the very antithesis of his father: charming and fun-loving whose love of London nightlife and married women annoyed and disappointed his morally upright parents. King George V expressed to his closest confidantes his concerns about the Prince of Wales and fears about his future. But then there were worries too about Bertie. King George was well aware of Bertie's uneven and sometimes volcanic temper, his shyness, and his struggles with his stuttering. But as the years passed, the Duke, thanks to his wife's steadfast support, grew more self-assured. This, plus the stable, happy family life presented by the Yorks gave King George confidence that should his second son ever be called to the throne, he and his wife would exercise their duties well. And in Lilibet, the King could see that this favored grandchild would likewise become one day, a conscientious Queen of England.

During the early 1930s, Lilibet's education began in earnest. She was educated like other girls of her station at the time and this meant being tutored by governesses. In 1933, a tall, Scottish woman, twenty-two-year-old Marion Crawford, who had been trained as a teacher, was appointed as governess to Princess Elizabeth and Princess Margaret. She came to be known as 'Crawfie' within the family and took on the responsibility of instructing Princess Elizabeth in a variety of subjects. Crawfie had discovered that Lilibet could already read, having been taught by her mother. "She proved an immensely interesting child to teach, with a high I.Q.," concluded Crawfie, "and from the start there was always about her a certain amenability, a reasonableness rare in anyone so very young. She was quick at picking anything up, and one never had to do a lot of explaining to her." Queen Mary was instrumental in ensuring that the Princess and her sister received a heavy dose of history, dynastic genealogies, as well as the geography of the Empire and Britain.

In the meantime, Britain in the early 1930s experienced economic and political instability. Ripples from the Wall Street Crash of 1929 had made their way across the Atlantic into Britain. Unemployment was a serious problem along with bankruptcies. In 1931, King George V promoted a National Government, a coalition of differing political parties headed by the Labour Prime Minister, Ramsay MacDonald. It was hoped that this coalition would tackle and succeed in addressing the disintegrating economic situation in Britain. All this was beyond the world of little Princess Elizabeth, whose focus during this time was understandably centered upon her parents, sister, loyal caretakers, and pets.

As the 1930s progressed and the little Princesses grew, it became obvious that Elizabeth was the more serious of the two and Margaret the more outgoing and artistic. Margaret early on showed an ear for music and a gift for mimicry. Listening to Elizabeth's French lessons from the door, little Margaret could mimic the accent so well that she exceeded her sister's attempts at her French pronunciations. Margaret became naturally competitive and this challenged Crawfie in her attempts to education the two sisters simultaneously.

Life for Princess Elizabeth and her sister was largely devoid of the presence of children their age. Sometimes they would play with their Lascelles male cousins (sons of the Princess Royal, the Duke of York's only sister) or they might occasionally meet with some of their cousins on their mother's side of the family, but for the most part it was Crawfie, their parents, Alah, and Margaret Macdonald, Princess Elizabeth's nursery-maid (referred to as 'Bobo' by the family) who surrounded Lilibet and Margaret as they grew. Life continued to revolve around 145 Piccadilly in London and at Royal Lodge in Windsor Great Park, a pink-tinged Regency villa dotted with the colorful blooms of rhododendrons. Weekends at Royal Lodge were a delight for Elizabeth and Margaret Rose. They ran and skipped amidst sweet fragrant hyacinths and azaleas, while all around them, birds chirped. But above all, it was a charming edifice that beckoned Lilibet and Margaret to the grounds of Royal Lodge. A thatched cottage, *Y Bwthyn Bach* ('The Little House') had been constructed for them on the grounds. The cottage, a gift from the Welsh people to the little Princesses, was built to scale for a child, forcing adults to get on their knees when they entered the abode. Here, Elizabeth and Margaret kept house, gave tea to their guests, giving the girls a chance to practice their domestic skills.

Besides enjoying playing at *Y Bwthyn Bach*, Lilibet and Margaret immersed themselves in a world full of animals. Animals were an integral part of Princess Elizabeth's world. Like her great-great-grandmother, Queen Victoria, Lilibet adored dogs. Her love of a particular breed of dogs, the corgis, became well-established early in life, beginning with Dookie, her family's first corgi. The hardy breed with the long body and short legs, large ears and endearing face, became a favorite of Lilibet's since childhood. Horses were another favored animal that Elizabeth came to know since childhood. King George V encouraged a love for horses in the toddler Lilibet. He had shown her his horses at Sandringham and "knew how engrossed she was in their care, their silky feel, their look and smell, the sound of their clopping hooves and of their snorts and neighs and winnies." Lilibet took her first riding lessons when she was four on a Shetland pony named Peggy, given to her by King George V; and in her nursery, among Elizabeth's favorite playthings were her stuffed horses which she rode and unsaddled every night. Even Crawfie was not immune from Elizabeth's obsession with horses, for the Princess would harness her governess and take her for a 'ride.' There came a point where Lilibet would even get up from bed to ensure that her toy ponies were lined up in good order, part of the child's obsession with tidiness which her governess, Crawfie noted.

In November 1934, Lilibet's paternal uncle, Prince George, the Duke of Kent, married the elegant Princess Marina of Greece. Dressed in tulle and satin, eight-year-old Elizabeth was one of the younger bridesmaids and behaved impeccably during the wedding ceremony held at Westminster Abbey. Princess Margaret Rose was not a member of the bridal part, being only four years old at the time.

The four-year age gap between Elizabeth and Margaret was not allowed to separate them in the classroom. This presented a challenge for Crawfie when it came to teaching the two sisters, but she managed it nonetheless. The Duchess of York did not allow the girls' age-gap to keep them apart. They were consequently dressed alike and grew up together. Photographs of the family during these years showed the two sisters, their dark brown hair cut short, dressed in identical outfits. Both girls were dressed as such - in pink coats and pink hats - for King George V's Silver Jubilee celebration.

Princess Elizabeth's venerable grandfather celebrated the Silver Jubilee of his reign in May 1935. He had lost some of his blustery personality, owing to his illness seven years before which had taken "the elasticity out him" so that "his quarter-deck manner, loud voice and thunderous rages" had been tempered. In celebration of the King's Silver Jubilee, a service of thanksgiving was held at St. Paul's Cathedral in London. Back at Buckingham Palace, King George and Queen Mary appeared on the balcony, accompanied by their granddaughter, Elizabeth, waving to the crowds below. King George had been taken aback by the manifestations of loyalty and admitted that, "I am beginning to think, that they must really like me for myself."

In November of King George's Jubilee year, when Lilibet was nine years old, the wedding took place at Westminster Abbey of the King's third son, Prince Henry, Duke of Gloucester, to Lady Alice Montagu-Douglas-Scott, a daughter of the Duke of Buccleuch. Again, Princess Elizabeth was chosen as a bridesmaid. This time was Princess Margaret was chosen as a bridesmaid as well. Both were dressed in frothy knee-length dresses with garlands of flowers on their heads. Queen Mary thought that "Lilibet & Margaret looked too sweet." After the wedding the bridal couple appeared on the balcony of

Buckingham Palace and when the time came for them to leave, Lilibet was in the palace forecourt waving good-bye. In a photograph of the event, the nine-year-old girl can be seen standing next to Princess Beatrice, the seventy-eight-year old youngest child of Queen Victoria.

Several weeks after the wedding, the Duchess of York was felled by a serious bout of influenza and was bedridden in Royal Lodge. While the Duchess was quarantined, the Duke took his daughters to the royal family's Sandringham estate in Norfolk for the family's traditional Christmas celebrations. While convalescing, the Duchess wrote to her elder daughter, saying: "My Darling Lilibet it seems a long time since I last saw you and Margaret …" The ailing mother urges Elizabeth to practice the piano and added that, "I hope you are having a lovely time in Sandringham, and being very polite to everybody."

During this time, Lilibet's Uncle David, the Prince of Wales, had begun a relationship with an American woman by the name of Wallis Simpson. King George and Queen Mary disapproved of Mrs. Simpson and could not understand their eldest son's infatuation with the married woman who also happened to be a divorcee. King George V was so incensed at the burgeoning romance that toward the end of 1934, he passionately exclaimed: "I pray to God my eldest son will never marry and have children, and that nothing will come between Bertie and Lilibet and the throne." Even more ominous and dramatic words had been expressed by the concerned King to his Prime Minister, Stanley Baldwin: "After I am dead, the boy will ruin himself within 12 months."

Not long after he spoke those words, King George V, 'Grandpapa England,' as he had been to Lilibet, died at Sandringham on January 20, 1936 at the age of seventy. The Times had summed up the late King's tenure on the British throne: "No reign has ever been fuller of national suffering, triumph, and disappointment, no monarch could have led his people with greater insight into their varying needs or with steadier devotion to the largest interests of the whole Empire. None strove more manfully beneath the burden of war nor carried the cause of peace nearer to his heart."

Lilibet was shaken by the death of her beloved grandfather. She watched in silent awe at some of the funereal ceremonies held in his honor. The Princess, dressed in black, had been taken by Crawfie on a gray and cold day to see the late King's coffin arrive in London from Sandringham to Paddington Station. Lilibet accompanied her parents to Westminster Hall, where in the cavernous and historic building, she witnessed King George V's lying-in-state. The nine-year-old Princess was impressed by the spectacle: the King's four sons in uniform surrounded the four corners of the coffin, standing guard, their heads bowed in reverence. Lilibet later commented to governess of the spectacle: "Uncle David was there, and he never moved at all, Crawfie. Not even an eyelid. It was wonderful. And everyone was so quiet. As if the King were asleep."

With the death of George V, his eldest son and heir, David, was proclaimed King Edward VIII. Edward VIII's association with Mrs. Simpson continued unabated as the months passed. In an era in which divorce was frowned upon, especially by the Church of England, of which the monarch was the titular head, Edward VIII's adulterous affair with a married woman caused a sensational scandal. The King's mother, Queen Mary, had succinctly summed up the dilemma Edward faced in having to choose the throne or Mrs. Simpson, when she said, "he is not responsible to himself alone."

Lilibet and Margaret met Mrs. Simpson in the spring of 1936, when, at the height of her romance with their uncle, Wallis Simpson, visited the Duke and Duchess of York with the King.

Edward VIII wanted to show off his new American station wagon to his brother and drove the short distance with Wallis from his home, Fort Belvedere, in Windsor Great Park, to Royal Lodge. Upon arriving at Royal Lodge, Wallis saw the contrast in the two brothers, the King "all enthusiasm and volubility" and the Duke "quiet, shy." Of the Duchess of York, Wallis wrote, "her justly famous charm was highly evident." And as for ten-year-old Elizabeth and five-year-old Margaret, their future aunt-by-marriage was struck by them, how both were "so beautifully mannered, so brightly scrubbed, that they might have stepped straight from the pages of a picture book." Wallis added that while "the Duke of York was sold on the American station wagon, the Duchess was not sold on David's other American interest [meaning herself]."

By November, Lilibet could sense the gloom that was pervasive among her relations, an ominous feeling that stemmed from the fact that King Edward's scandalous affair with Wallis Simpson was coming to a head. The Duchess of York and Queen Mary were a bundle of nerves, but the one most anxious was Lilibet's father, the Duke of York. If his brother were not allowed to marry Wallis, then what? The burden of the throne would inevitably fall upon him and then Lilibet. The strain on Lilibet's parents was such that that the Duchess of York likened it to "sitting on the edge of a volcano."

Everything finally came to a head when, seeing that he could not overcome the political opposition to his intention of marrying Wallis Simpson and remaining King and Emperor at the same time, Edward VIII chose to abdicate in favor of his brother, the Duke of York. The instrument of abdication was signed on December 10, 1936 at Fort Belvedere, witnessed by David's younger brothers, Albert, Henry, and George – the Dukes of York, Gloucester, and Kent.

In his speech explaining to the British Empire, his decision to abdicate, the former King Edward VIII talked of the confidence he had in his brother, the new King George VI, and of the family life he and the new Queen Elizabeth and their daughters shared: "This decision has been made less difficult to me by the sure knowledge that my brother, with his long training the public affairs of this Country and with his fine qualities, will be able to take my place forthwith without interruption or injury to the life and progress of the Empire, and he has one matchless blessing, enjoyed by so many of you, and not bestowed on me, a happy home with his wife and children." The former Edward VIII ended his broadcast with the words, "God save The King."

Lilibet's father was King; she was now only a heartbeat away from becoming Queen of England. Lilibet was first in line in the succession, the Heiress Presumptive to the British throne.

On the afternoon of the abdication, outside 145 Piccadilly, a crowd had gathered, garnering the attention of Lilibet. When she asked a footman what the commotion was about, he told her that her uncle had abdicated the throne. Lilibet rushed to Margaret to tell her the stunning news.

"Does that mean you will have to be the next queen?" said Princess Margaret.

"Yes, some day," came Princess Elizabeth's reply.

"Poor you," said Margaret.

ILLUSTRATIONS

The Duchess of Kent with 'Drina,' a young Princess
Victoria. Portrait by Henry Bone, c. 1824 (public domain)

Queen Victoria receives the news of her accession, June 20, 1837 by Henry Tanworth Wells, c.1887 (public domain)\
Kensington Palace in London where Queen Victoria was born and where she spent her childhood years.
(source:ahill 88 via pixabay CC0)

Kensington Palace in London where Queen Victoria was born and where she spent her childhood years.
(source:ahill 88 via pixabay CC0)

Three Generations—The Queen, the Duchess of York, Princess Elizabeth, Prince George

A photograph of the young 'Lilibet' – Princess Elizabeth with her parents, the future King George VI and Queen Elizabeth, and her paternal grandmother, Queen Mary. (The Miriam and Ida D. Wallach Division of Art, Prints and Photographs: Print Collection, The New York Public Library. "Three Generations – The Queen, the Duchess of York, Princess Elizabeth, Prince George" New York Public Library Digital Collections. Accessed December 30, 2018. http://digitalcollections.nypl.org/items/5e66b3e8-9156-d471-e040-e00a180654d7)

H.R.H. Princess Elizabeth in the Auxiliary Territorial Service, April 1945 (Detail from: The Imperial War Museums, Ministry of Information Second Official Photographer. https://commons.wikimedia.org/wiki/File:Hrh_Princess_Elizabeth_in_the_Auxiliary_Territorial _Service,_April_1945_TR2832.jpg. Accessed December 30, 2018.

H.R.H. Princess Elizabeth and her husband H.R.H. the Duke of Edinburgh, c. 1952. (Detail from National Film Board of Canada Still Photography Division [graphic material] (R1106-14-7-E), Library and Archives Canada, Item No. K-2805, Accession No. 1971-271 NPC, Droits d'Auteur: Expiré)

Chapter 5. Victoria: "I will be good"

I n March 1830, Princess Victoria sat for a history lesson with Baroness Lehzen and found that a page had been slipped into *Howlett's Tables* of the Kings and Queens of England. The page contained a genealogical table that showed just how close to the throne Victoria was. Upon seeing the inserted pages, the Princess said to Lehzen, "I never saw that before."

"No, Princess," said Lehzen.

Upon studying the genealogical table, Princess Victoria exclaimed, "I am nearer to the throne than I thought." A flood of tears poured forth from Victoria who then declared, "I will be good."

Princess Victoria, always a good pupil, continued to progress in her lessons. She spoke French and German well and excelled in arithmetic. She also continued to improve her drawing skills. The Princess was given dancing and singing lessons and "had a soprano voice, not powerful but remarkably sweet and true." Victoria was instructed by the Reverend Davys in religion and brought up on the precepts of the Church of England. The quality of the Princess's education was analyzed when the Bishops of London and Lincoln as well as the Archbishop of Canterbury examined Victoria prior to her eleventh birthday. The Archbishop was pleased at how well the Princess was progressing. He found that Victoria "appears well versed in the chronology and accession of the Kings and Queens of England ... and acquainted with many particulars both of ancient and French history."

Satisfied to see that her daughter had passed her examinations, the Duchess of Kent wrote to Victoria for her eleventh birthday in 1830, urging her to continue to do well, telling the Princess that, "should it be the will of Providence ... that if you be called to fill the highest Station in the Country, - you will shew yourself worthy of it; - and that you will not disappoint the hopes of your anxious Mother! – then, only then, can you be happy and make others happy."

Part of the education of Princess Victoria included advice from her uncle, Prince Leopold. In 1831, he became King Leopold I of the Belgians and it was from Brussels that Leopold wrote to Victoria, dispensing sage advice to his niece, for which the Princess would come to be grateful for. King

Leopold began to tutor the Princess in how to be a successful monarch by writing to Victoria on her thirteenth birthday, in which "he urged her to give close attention in future to serious matters." And on Victoria's fourteenth birthday, King Leopold "reflected much on her character, and gave her good advice as to its development." Leopold highlighted two wise observations: "Nothing is stronger and clearer evidence of an unfitness for great and high enterprises than a mind that is taken up with trifles. Soundness of mind must show itself in distinguishing between the important and unimportant." King Leopold, whom Victoria referred to as her "dearest uncle" who had always been "like a father" to her, found an apt pupil in his niece. Princess Victoria could not have asked for a better mentor than King Leopold, who in effect, took on the role of a surrogate father. Leopold was intelligent and astute, and possessed great political acumen.

King Leopold insisted to Victoria that "history is the most important study for you." The King brought up negative examples from the history of France of how not to rule.

Princess Victoria noted this trend and eventually asked her uncle, having learned "what a

Queen ought *not* to be, that you will send me what a Queen *ought* to be."

The Duchess of Kent had no qualms about Victoria being influenced by King Leopold. But as for cultivating connections and relationships with the British royal family, the Duchess continued to keep Princess Victoria away from court as much as possible. The less her daughter mixed with the dissolute Hanoverian family, the better for the child and for her image. This was, after all, part of the Kensington System, which had as one of its purposes, the cultivation of an unimpeachable image of the Princess Victoria.

During Victoria's formative years, Britain was proceeding apace in technological advancements. In 1830, the first commercial service involving the Liverpool and Manchester Railways began. The next year, Michael Faraday paved the way for electric engines and generators with his discovery of electro-magnetic currents. And in 1834, Charles Babbage designed the Analytical Engine, a forerunner of the computer. British politics also had undergone changes during this time. Agitated segments of the population flirted openly with republicanism, making them a menace to the throne. There were fears of revolution if the franchise was not expanded. In 1832, the Reform Act was passed by Parliament which expanded the vote to nearly eighteen percent of the male population of England and Wales. The more liberal minded party, the Whigs, were for such changes, but the conservative Tories, were opposed. The Duchess of Kent and Conroy were Whig supporters while King William and Queen Adelaide were staunch Tories. This political difference between Kensington Palace and the court exacerbated the strained relations between Princess Victoria's mother and her brother and sister-in-law, the King and Queen.

King William's ten illegitimate children were also a source of aggravation for the Duchess of Kent. The Duchess told Victoria's governess, the Duchess of Northumberland, that, "I never did, neither will I ever associate Victoria in any way with the illegitimate members of the Royal family; with the King they die ... how would it be possible to teach Victoria the difference between vice and virtue?"

In 1832 when Princess Victoria was thirteen, she began a series of 'Royal Progresses' throughout her future kingdom that continued for several years. These trips through Britain, devised by Conroy, had the object of introducing Victoria to her future subjects and exposing the Princess to different parts of Britain. Victoria also began to write in her diary, a habit which she would continue for the rest of her life. She inscribed the first volume, dated the 31st of July 1832, with the words: "This Book Mamma gave me that I might write the journal of my journey to Wales in it. Victoria."

The first trip was a success. The Princess, accompanied by her mother and Conroy, was enthusiastically welcomed during her visits which encompassed the coal-mining areas of North Wales to Chester and Derbyshire, and on to Oxford. In replying to an address by the Vice-Chancellor in the Sheldonian Theatre of Oxford University, the Duchess of Kent said:

> *We close a most interesting journey by a visit to this University, that the Princess may see, as far as her years will allow, all that is interesting in it. The history of our country has taught her to know its importance by the many distinguished persons who, by their character and talents, have been raised been raised to eminence by the education they have received in it. Your loyalty to the King and recollection of the favour you have enjoyed under the paternal sway of his house, could not fail, I was sure,*

to lead you to receive his niece with all the disposition you evince to make this visit agreeable and instructive to her. It is my object to ensure, by all means in my power, her being so educated as to meet the just expectation of all classes in this great and free country.

The next year, Victoria noted in her journal, "I am today fourteen years old! How *very old*." The Princess still lacked a circle of young friends her age, and she yearned for such company, but the Kensington System forbade such pleasures. Though Victoire Conroy was consorted with Victoria, the Princess never took to her. Instead, she preferred the company of the animals around her, especially her cherished Dash, a charming silky-haired King Charles spaniel. Dash been given by Sir John Conroy to the Duchess of Kent but was quickly adopted by Princess Victoria as her own. "DEAR SWEET LITTLE DASH," as the Princess referred to her cherished pet, was doted upon by his royal owner in periodically in blue trousers and scarlet jacket.

The Royal Progresses continued in 1833 when Princess Victoria visited the Isle of Wight, Plymouth, Torquay, and Exeter. King William IV was opposed to these 'Royal Progresses' but did not prevent them from taking place. The years had not eased the strain between King William and the Duchess of Kent and so the friction that marred relations between Kensington Palace and the King's court continued unabated. Even a solemn and important ceremony such as Princess Victoria's 1835 confirmation in the Church of England did not deter the King from letting his feud with the Duchess of Kent go unheeded. Sir John Conroy had been invited to attend the religious ceremony but King William did not want the Duchess of Kent's confidante present and ordered him to leave. Victoria herself was moved by having undergone the confirmation, and upon hearing the Archbishop's words on her future responsibilities, Victoria "drowned in tears and [was] frightened to death." Victoria wrote in her journal: "I was very much affected indeed when we came home."

No doubt Princess Victoria's frayed nerves had contributed to this reaction. At home, the Kensington System continued to exact a toll on her. The Duchess of Kent was under Sir John Conroy's complete sway and only Baroness Lehzen could offer Victoria the refuge she sought in her embattled home where she and her mother were at loggerheads. Not surprisingly, Princess Victoria's health suffered. She endured headaches and colds and other such ailments but above all, it was her nerves which suffered the most. The Duchess of Kent tried to mitigate the situation by asking Baron Stockmar, (who was in London in 1834) for his help. The wise doctor replied that it was not possible to remedy the situation. He told the Duchess that, "it seems to me" that the problem lay "much more in the Princess herself and Sir John Conroy. The latter seems to me to be an excellent business man and absolutely devoted to your Royal Highness. But how can I overlook that he is vain, ambitious, most sensitive and most hot tempered?" Stockmar, in analyzing the situation where Princess Victoria was concerned, added: "Wherever she looked in the house, she encountered Sir John as the sole regulator of the whole machine. As soon as she felt something unpleasant in the house ... she recognised the main cause of it in the person of Sir John. Such impressions go deepest at a youthful age ... With every day the Princess grew up ... she became resentful of what must have looked to her as an exercise of undue control over herself ... Your Royal Highness has agreed with me that Sir John's personal behaviour towards the Princess has been apt only too often to worsen this state of affairs." Baron Stockmar's words of wisdom to the Duchess of Kent ended with a plea: "May Your Royal Highness not do anything that could *produce coldness and distance between you and the Princess*, neither *now nor in the future*."

Chapter 6. Elizabeth: Heiress Presumptive

With the abdication of King Edward VIII on December 10, 1936, the burden of kingship had fallen squarely on Princess Elizabeth's father. This burden was best encapsulated by Wallis Simpson when she saw its impacts on Edward VIII upon his accession. She wrote that "he had become the prisoner of his heritage."

The new King, who took the name of George VI in honor of his father, had always been in his elder brother's dazzling shadow. Bertie had always felt that "his oldest brother possessed a star quality that he felt he lacked." Even Crawfie noted of George VI when he was Duke of York and living at 145 Piccadilly, that he had a "boyish appearance and delicate look" who "was not considered to be a particularly important person in the family." As for the public, they knew him largely "by virtue of a medium that did not flatter him." Bertie's public speeches were recorded, and they showed his stuttering and stammering. Only thanks to long months under the tutelage of Lionel Logue, an Australian speech therapist, did Bertie finally overcome his speech impediment. But with the pressures of being King, there was every possibility that his speech problems could return. The realization that the responsibilities of kingship had fallen on him hit the new King hard. When he arrived at Marlborough House, the London home of Queen Mary, the new King wept on his mother's shoulder. Queen Mary confided in her diary of her shock of "David's abdication of the Throne of his Empire because he wishes to marry Mrs. Simpson!!!!! … It is a terrible blow to us all & particularly to poor Bertie."

King George VI, who had always relied on the strength and support of his wife, now turned to her more than ever. At his Accession Council two days after the abdication, George VI, alluded to this when he said: "With My wife and helpmate by My side, I take up the heavy task which lies before Me."

The Archbishop of Canterbury had expressed his confidence in the new Queen Elizabeth, stating that, "King George will have at his side the gentle strength and quiet wisdom of a wife who has already endeared herself to all by her grace, her charm, her bright and eager kindliness of heart."

As for Princess Elizabeth, the immensity of the new title assumed by her parents hit her when she saw an envelope addressed to 'Her Majesty the Queen.' "That's *Mummie* now, isn't it?" And when asked by Princess Margaret if this all meant that she was to become Queen of England one day, Elizabeth replied: "Yes, I suppose it does." And when Crawfie told the two sisters that they were to move to Buckingham Palace, Lilibet and Margaret looked at their governess "in horror."

"What!" said Lilibet to Crawfie. "You mean forever?"

The accession of her father as King George VI meant that Princess Elizabeth became first in line to the throne at the age of ten. And though Elizabeth had become the 'Heiress Presumptive,' she had never been ambitious to become the next monarch. On the contrary, it was said that Lilibet "used to pray for God to send her 'a little brother' – in much the same spirit that Princess Victoria wished for her aunt Queen Adelaide to produce a living heir to William IV."

The trauma of the Abdication Crisis was such that it was never discussed within the family. The Duke and Duchess of Windsor, as David and Wallis had become (with Wallis being denied the honor of being a Royal Highness), became *personae non gratae* to the royals. As for the new monarchs and their daughters, duty called them and this meant on a basic level, that they had to move house. The family moved out of 145 Piccadilly and into the imposing Buckingham Palace, with its grand formal rooms and long corridors. Crawfie recalled settling in to their new home:

> *It took us quite a while to settle down and get the old routine going again. I think we all rather felt we were camping in a desert. The house in Piccadilly had been so comfortable and quite small. Visitors had been mostly personal friends, and even they had been few and far between. The palace was always full of people coming and going. With its post office, secretaries, privy purse and all the rest of it, it was more like a village than a home.*

Despite the grandeur of their new home, life went on as normal for Lilibet and Margaret. Lessons continued with Crawfie. These lessons were augmented by trips with the girls' formidable grandmother, Queen Mary, to museums and historic places like the British Museum, Hampton Court, and the Tower of London. Princess Elizabeth politely followed and listened to her grandmother as Queen Mary explained the significance of the places they visited and of the things they saw. Princess Margaret was an eager student, a chatter box who earned her grandmother's approval in her curiosity.

Elizabeth and Margaret continued to remain close, but inevitably rivalries arose between the two siblings. The coronation of King George VI and Queen Elizabeth in May 1937 was a case in point. The King decided that both his daughters would wear lace dresses in white with dark purple velvet trains edged in ermine. When Margaret learned that Lilibet's train was to be longer than hers by a foot, the younger sister objected vehemently. Margaret's forthright character and competitive spirit burst to the fore when it came to what she was to wear for the coronation.

In order to prepare the sisters for the coronation, a large panorama of King George IV's coronation in 1821 had been placed in the girls' schoolroom at Buckingham Palace. Queen Mary gave them lectures on the historic significance of such an event, so that when the time came for their parents' own crowning, Elizabeth and Margaret would understand as much as possible what was to unfold before their eyes.

On May 12, 1937, Princess Elizabeth recorded her impressions of her parents' coronation, dedicating it with the words, "To Mummy and Papa. In Memory of Their Coronation from Lilibet by Herself."

Elizabeth and Margaret, looking every inch the royal princess that they were, rode in the cool rain in a carriage they shared with their paternal aunt, the Princess Royal, and her teenage son. Margaret was "nodding with half sleep within her carriage, and her elder sister, sparkling with delight and waving to the groups of schoolchildren which she passed." When the procession of the King and Queen came along, there was "an army of gold and scarlet, passing along the wide streets like a flame, before the state coach drawn by eight grey horses." In the coach, the King and Queen, resplendent in their coronation attire, acknowledged with graceful waves, the cheers of their subjects.

To the fanfare of trumpets and music, Princess Elizabeth's father was welcomed to the historic and hallowed Westminster Abbey. She heard shouts of 'God Save King George' reverberating around her. And as the coronation ceremony unfolded, Lilibet watched as the Archbishop of Canterbury give her father the Orb from the altar and say, "remember that the whole world is subject to the Power and Empire of Christ our Redeemer." Then there was the supreme moment when the Archbishop crowned the George VI with St. Edward's Crown. "The cry of *God Save the King* rang through the nave, it went out, growing in strength to the streets. Trumpets sounded, piercing and triumphant ... The bells of Westminster rang ... and then, far away at the other end of the metropolis, beside the ancient waters of the Thames, the guns from the Tower of London boomed over the city."

The coronation had an impact on Princess Elizabeth, who wrote: "I thought it all VERY, VERY wonderful ... The arches and beams at the top [of the abbey] were covered with a sort of haze of wonder as Papa was crowned, at least I thought so."

The coronation service was long, and when at last in the program Lilibet saw the word 'Finis,' she and Queen Mary exchanged a knowing look, the Princess relieved that the end had finally arrived. After the coronation, the royal family returned to Buckingham Palace where they made the obligatory balcony appearance, still dressed in their coronation finery. Lilibet looked every inch the princess that she was, with her lace dress, ermine-edged velvet robe, and coronet.

Life returned to a routine after the coronation. Lessons again, and a Girl Guide troop to which Elizabeth belonged, occupied her time. She was also being exposed more to public engagements in preparation for her future. At home, domestic life remained on an even keel, but on the international front, concerns about Adolf Hitler's plans for Europe preoccupied many. In 1936, German troops had marched into the Rhineland. In March 1938, the Anschluss took place whereby Nazi Germany annexed Austria. This was followed by the Sudetenland Crisis in October in which the Czech Sudetenland was ceded to Germany in order to appease Hitler. Clearly, the winds of war were blowing and tensions on the European Continent were causing many political leaders, including the British, much cause for concern.

Should war erupt, help and cooperation from the U.S. would be necessary for Britain to win. And so, with war looming on the horizon, King George VI and Queen Elizabeth departed on a six-week tour of Canada and the United States. The royal family, including Queen Mary with Princess Elizabeth and Princess Margaret were at Southampton to bid the King and Queen farewell as they sailed off on the *Empress of Australia*. Queen Mary recorded in her diary an exchange between her two granddaughters which illustrates the sense of propriety and duty that Princess Elizabeth had: "Margaret said, 'I have my handkerchief' & Lilibet asnd. [answered] 'To wave, not to cry' – which I thought charming."

On board the *Empress of Australia*, Queen Elizabeth wrote to Princess Elizabeth: "My Darling Lilibet … I hated saying goodbye to you & Margaret, but know that you will be happy with Miss C & Alah …Goodbye my Angel, give Margaret a HUGE kiss, & an ENORMOUS one for yourself from Your ever loving Mummy…"

In Canada, the King and Queen were greeted by large crowds everywhere they went. They traversed the vast country, arriving at the end of May in Alberta. From there, hints of uneasy sibling relations are hinted at in a letter Queen Elizabeth wrote to Princess Elizabeth from the Banff Springs Hotel. Surrounded by the majestic Rockies, the Queen, who described the mountains as "very beautiful" went on to add about Princess Margaret, "you musn't forget that she is really very little, & sometimes you must control yourself when she is a little teasing. I know it is difficult, but you can do it, & I know you will." Crawfie had expressed concerns that Lilibet was too castigating toward Margaret, and hence the words of advice from Queen Elizabeth. To mitigate her reprimanding tone, the Queen added in her postscript, references to the family pet corgi: "A nice pat for Dookie please. In one of the papers here there was a picture of you & M with Dookie, & it said 'an old Corgi of uncertain temper!! Poor old Dookie."

By this stage in Princess Elizbeth's life it was evident that she differed highly in character from her sister, Margaret. They were like chalk and cheese; and this difference in character and outlook between the two sisters never changed. The Countess of Airlie, who knew the family well, noted that Princess Elizabeth "seemed to me one of the most unselfish girls I had even met … I thought that no two sisters could have been less alike than the Princesses, the elder with her quiet simplicity, the younger with her puckish expression and irrepressible high spirits…" Crawfie recalled how: "Of the two children, Lilibet was the one with the temper, but it was under control. Margaret was often naughty…" Moreover, Lilibet "had always the more dignity of the two." In fact, "Lilibet was far more strictly disciplined than Margaret ever was." Crawfie recalled that "the King set a very high standard for Lilibet … The King had great pride in her, and she in turn had, inborn, this desire to do what was expected of her."

When Princess Elizabet was thirteen, her education was supplemented with tutoring from Henry Marten, the Vice-Provost of Eton, who taught the Princess constitutional history. While on board the *Empress of Australia* as it neared Canada and cruised past large icebergs, Queen Elizabeth brought up the subject of these tutoring sessions, telling her daughter that, "I <u>do</u> hope that you are enjoying your Saturday evenings with Mr. Marten – try & learn as much from him, & mark how he brings the human element into all of history – of course history <u>is</u> made by ordinary humans, & one must not forget that." Marten succeeded in bringing history to life for Lilibet. It was thanks to Marten that Princess Elizabeth "learnt to love and respect Queen Victoria, whose vast experience enabled her to influence policy in a perfectly constitutional way – such as bringing her beloved India under the crown, and persuading Disraeli to make her Queen-Empress."

The visit of King George VI and Queen Elizabeth to Canada and the United States was an unqualified success and upon their return they soon embarked on a brief visit to Dartmouth Naval College in July. The political tensions in Europe continued to remain high that summer of 1939, but on this special day, thirteen-year-old Princess Elizabeth's thoughts were focused on one of the naval cadets who had been assigned to entertain her and Margaret. He was Prince Philip of Greece, the nephew of Lord Louis Mountbatten, a great-grandson of Queen Victoria, and friend of the royal family.

Philip was the youngest child of Prince Andrew of Greece and his wife, Princess Alice of Battenberg, a granddaughter of Queen Victoria. Elizabeth and Philip were thus third cousins, having both descended from Queen Victoria. Though Philip was born in Corfu, Greece, to the Greek royal family, he did not have a drop of Greek blood, as the royal family descended from Prince William of Denmark who became King George I of Greece. Not long after Prince Philip's birth, the Greek royal family's fortunes fell, and Prince Andrew and his family fled Greece. Consequently, Prince Philip had been raised in exile in France and Britain. Philip's parents had divorced, his older sisters were already married and living in various parts of Europe and so Philip did not experience a stable family life, unlike Lilibet. His uncle, Lord Louis Mountbatten, had taken Philip under his wing and became a mentor. Naval life was a strong influence in the life of the Mountbattens. Lord Louis's father, Prince Louis of Battenberg, had been First Sea Lord, the head of Britain's Royal Navy. Lord Louis became a high-ranking naval officer himself, and so it came as no surprise to find that Prince Philip had chosen to pursue a career and serve in the Royal Navy.

When Lilibet met Philip that summer of 1939, he had just turned eighteen. He was tall, blond, handsome, and exhibited a casual, virile attitude that annoyed Crawfie but enthralled Lilibet. Crawfie admitted that at the time, Prince Philip was "rather like a Viking, with a sharp face and piercing blue eyes ... He was good-looking, though rather offhand in his manner." Philip showed off at the tennis courts, impressing Margaret and Lilibet with his prowess at jumping over the nets.

"How good he is, Crawfie," gushed Lilibet, who never stopped watching Philip. "How high he can jump."

Throughout the visit, the young Princess watched Philipp as he showed off on the tennis court, jumping over the net with no effort. She laughed at his jokes, gawked at his healthy appetite at lunch, and "ignored the awkward qualities that others found tiresome – his barking laugh, his brash, edgy bluntness, verging on rudeness, his tendency to dominate."

Philip never ceased to impress Lilibet that day at Dartmouth. From the moment she first laid eyes on the blue-eyed Prince until her last glimpse of him, Philip made a lasting impression on her. When Elizabeth, her sister and parents, sailed away on the River Dart on board the yacht, *Victoria and Albert*, her eyes were firmly fixed on one special naval cadet. Philip had rowed out onto the choppy waters of the River Dart in a small boat in pursuit of the royal yacht. Lilibet watched in rapt attention as the blond Viking rowed and rowed until he disappeared, the yacht having sped quickly away.

Chapter 7. Victoria: The Throne Beckons

Baron Stockmar's sage advice went unheeded by the Duchess of Kent. She still relied on Sir John Conroy's advice and so Princess Victoria's nemesis remained in his undisputed position as comptroller and adviser to the Duchess of Kent. The Princess's 'imprisonment' in Kensington Palace continued unabated.

To the Princess's annoyance, Sir John Conroy continued to have a significant role in her mother's household. He accompanied the Duchess and Princess as Victoria embarked on another Royal Progress in England. These journeys exhausted Victoria, who was met by large crowds. The visits were full of entertainments and official welcomes. During a stop at Burghley, the Princess and her mother were treated to splendid welcome by the civic authorities, where Victoria was lauded as one "destined to mount the throne of these realms." A ball was held in the Princess's honor as well, with three hundred invited guests, where the Princess danced one dance, and then retired to bed.

At the end of September in 1836, Victoria and the Duchess of Kent set off for a holiday in the Kent seaside town of Ramsgate. While there, the Princess was visited by King Leopold and his new wife, Queen Louise, daughter of France's King Louis Philippe. Princess Victoria took to her new youthful aunt who showered her with affection and gifts. King Leopold continued to ply his niece with wise words, with Victoria recording: "He gave me very valuable and important advice. We talked over many important and serious matters ... He has always treated me as his child and I love him most dearly for it."

In early October, Princess Victoria fell seriously ill with fever and a racing pulse. She lay ill for weeks in Ramsgate with septic tonsils. Baroness Lehzen nursed the Princess with devotion, earning Lehzen Victoria's eternal gratitude, recording in her diary that, "I can never sufficiently repay her for all she has borne and done for me. She is the *most affectionate*, _devoted, attached_ and _disinterested_ friend I have and I love her most dearly ..."

During this time of serious illness, Victoria had to contend with the ambitious Conroy who saw his chance in the weakened Princess, an opportunity to raise his standing. "Those large blue eyes staring out of the sunken face must be forced to look into the future." Here was Conroy's chance to make Princess Victoria sign a paper that would agree to making him her private secretary when she became Queen of England. In this Conroy had the Duchess of Kent's backing. Conroy approached the sickbed and shoved pen and paper at the weak and sickly Victoria to sign. She was adamant. She would not be intimidated. Princess Victoria refused to sign. Conroy had not contended with a willful girl who would not be coerced. In his attempt to get Princess Victoria to sign her future away, Sir John Conroy had overplayed his hand. In recounting the distasteful incident, the Princess merely wrote: "I resisted in spite of my illness."

The serious illness suffered by Princess Victoria eventually abated and by end of several weeks' convalescence, the residents of Ramsgate were gratified to find her and the Duchess of Kent taking in the brisk sea air during leisurely walks outdoors. When mother and daughter arrived back at Kensington Palace in January 1836, Princess Victoria was delighted to find that they were to move into new apartments – rooms that were more agreeable. With her health improving, Victoria began her lessons again which were on a more advanced level. She read all four volumes of Blackstone's *Commentaries on English Law* and English and French authors, with French works being read in that language. Friends were still non-existent for the Princess, her mother being stone-deaf to Baron Stockmar's suggestion that Victoria be allowed some companions of her age to keep her company.

It thus came as no surprise that Princess Victoria reveled in visits by cousins close to her age. In February, a set of such cousins, the Princes Ferdinand and Augustus of Saxe-Coburg-Kohary paid her a visit. Princess Victoria enjoyed her cousins' company, particularly when they partnered her in dances; and when they departed, a void had been left in Princess's life, whose passionate attachments to people and things were by now clearly evident. "Now they are quite gone," lamented the emotional Victoria when the brothers left in April, "& no one can replace them." Prince Ferdinand left England and made his way to Portugal to marry Victoria's contemporary, Queen Maria da Gloria, and become her consort, a marriage King Leopold promoted. Another marriage King Leopold sought was that of Princess Victoria to his other nephew, Prince Albert of Saxe-Coburg-Gotha. And it was to this end that King Leopold saw to it that

Prince Albert and his older brother, Prince Ernst, set foot on English soil not long after Ferdinand and Augustus left.

The question of Princess Victoria's future husband had occupied the thinking of not only King Leopold but also King William IV. Europe's prized heiress was of the age when marriage was not far off and whoever her husband might be was of vital importance, owing not only to the position he would take but also to the influential role he might likely have over his wife when she became Queen Victoria. Prince George of Cambridge, a cousin of Victoria's was a favored candidate as were the sons of the Dutch Prince of Orange who visited England. But Victoria never saw her cousin George in a romantic light and neither did she take a liking to the Dutch Princes, all of which boded well for King Leopold and his choice for Victoria, Prince Albert.

King William was incensed at the matrimonial machinations of King Leopold and ordered his Foreign Secretary, Lord Palmerston to tell the Duchess of Kent that she must not have her Coburg brother and his sons visit England. The Duchess wrote to Queen Adelaide, telling her sister-in-law that, "I really cannot … look at this visit as of any consequence or as entailing any difficulties, when I consider that it is not until three or four years hence that the Princess will be called upon to change her situation in life. Nor can I see any difference between my brother being accompanied by his sons to the Prince of Orange having brought his."

Clearly, the fractious relationship between the Duchess of Kent and King William IV had not subsided with the years. Though conflict and friction dominated Princess Victoria's life, there were also moments of delight, especially when it came to the arts. Victoria was allowed to visit the theater and watch plays, opera, and the ballet - visits which allowed her to cultivate her love of the arts. The Princess's interest was such that she filled her sketchbook with the stars and the shows that she had seen. Where Victoria's preferences lay was evident when she wrote in the mid-1830s, that, "I am not fond of Handel's music ... I must say I prefer the present Italian school such as Rossini, Bellini and Donizetti to anything else." The Princess was especially impressed by the soprano, Giulia Grisi, whom she considered a favorite. For her daughter's sixteenth birthday, the Duchess of Kent had invited to Kensington Palace, members of the Italian opera, to perform before Victoria. Grisi sang as did the famed Luigi Lablache. Victoria thought Lablache's voice to be "immensely powerful." Of her special birthday present, the Princess recorded that, "I stayed up till twenty minutes past one. I was MOST EXCEEDINGLY DELIGHTED." The Duchess agreed to let Lablache give Victoria singing lessons, which again, delighted the Princess no end.

By this time, Princess Victoria had grown into a slight girl, not tall in the least, with brown hair and large blue eyes. A glimpse into how she presented herself to the world could be gleaned by a contemporary newspaper description of the Princess as she sat in the royal box, watching a performance:

> *There is a tone of character about her that is very delightful ... with the look and pleasurable expression of a child, she has a sedate aspect which is promising in one who is probably destined to fill a throne. A sweet smile sometimes played over her features, and illuminated for a moment the languor they take when they are at rest. Occasionally a charming colour mounted to her cheeks, naturally wan, and flushed them with a glow of sudden delight, then it rapidly subsided, and her fair hair, round face and her eyes .... which have the placid beauty of the dove's and her*

delicately outlined mouth fell into
that tranquility which seems to be her
natural temperament.

When Princess Victoria turned seventeen in 1836, this meant that within a year upon reaching her majority at eighteen, she would be able to ascend the throne without the need for a regent. But for time being, she was still underage and if King William died, then the Duchess of Kent was still to act as regent for her daughter.

As the King aged, his patience grew thinner and his "self-control diminished, while his jealousy of his prerogatives as Monarch increased." Instead of treating King William with deference, Victoria's mother continued to antagonize him with her tactlessness. Things came to a spectacular head during the birthday celebrations for King William at Windsor Castle in August 1836, an event which erupted in a scandalous scene that shocked the Princess and mortified the distinguished guests.

Chapter 8. Elizabeth: The War Years

In August 1939, Princess Elizabeth and her family were in Balmoral on holiday. The large estate by the banks of the River Dee, had been the royal family's Scottish home since the days of Queen Victoria. For Lilibet and Margaret, Balmoral offered them endless delights: "riding their ponies across the heather-covered hillsides; the thrilling roaring of stags and the plaintive 'go-back, go-back' of grouse calling from the heather; the enormous teas with shrimps and scones, baps and bannocks; and, most exciting of all, the seven pipers who would march around the dining room after dinner." The family's Balmoral idyll was halted, however, when King George VI rushed back to London on August 23rd as war loomed on the horizon. A week later, Queen Elizabeth joined the King. Elizabeth and Margaret with Crawfie were left in Scotland, staying at Birkhall, eight miles from Balmoral itself. Then, on September 1st, Hitler's troops invaded Poland. In the space of only twenty-one years, Britain was again at war. King George broadcast a speech to the Empire, telling his subjects that they were united in the face of the dark days before them. Upon hearing of the troubles, nine-year-old Princess Margaret, perplexed at what was unfolding, asked: "Who is this Hitler spoiling everything?" As for Queen Elizabeth, who understood the full gravity of the situation, she was "stunned" at the thought that they were about to embark on full-scale war.

From London, Queen Elizabeth gave instructions to Crawfie that Elizabeth and Margaret were to continue receiving lessons. For three months they stayed on in Scotland. The girls were reunited with their parents at Sandringham for Christmas and then the sisters were sent to Royal Lodge while the King and Queen stayed in London. When Hitler's troops invaded Denmark and Norway in April 1940, and then the Low Countries, the war took a dramatic, much more active and sinister turn. Britain was clearly on target for invasion, which meant that the Princesses were vulnerable. It was suggested that Elizabeth and Margaret be evacuated and sent to Canada. After all, other reigning royal families were going into exile and countless British children were being sent abroad for their safety as well. In reply to this suggestion, Queen Elizabeth declared emphatically: "The children could not go without me, I could not possibly leave the King, and the King would never go."

The question of where the Princesses should live was finally settled in May 1940 when they were sent with Crawfie to live at Windsor Castle. To the public, the whereabouts of the Princesses were a mystery; they were told that Elizabeth and Margaret were living 'somewhere in the country,' a fate shared by countless British children who had been sent from London to the countryside. Windsor Castle, with its centuries old ties to English history had been home to countless monarchs including Queen Victoria, who secluded herself here for years after the death of her husband, Prince Albert in 1861. With its forbidding towers and thick gray walls, the castle took on an even more grim atmosphere with black out curtains reducing the already low light the residents had to contend with from small light bulbs. The Princesses stayed at the Lancaster Tower in two bedrooms: Lilibet, as usual, with Bobo MacDonald; and Margaret, as usual, with Alah. Life at Windsor Castle was without ostentation. Many of the valuable paintings, rugs, chandeliers, and *objets d'art* had been carefully stored away. Fuel cuts meant that rooms could be icy cold. Air raid sirens meant that Lilibet and Margaret had to grab their gas masks and rush down to the shelter. Outside, the fields surrounding the castle were ploughed so that crops could be grown for food.

May 1940 was also marked by Winston Churchill becoming Prime Minister. Several days after taking the reins of government, Churchill gave his stirring speech in which he declared, 'we shall never surrender.' Churchill's oratorial and leadership skills, along with King George VI's inspiring guidance helped to buoy the spirits of the nation, which were direly needed as Nazi Germany began a campaign in September 1940 of intense bombing, targeting mainly London. The terrifying raids came to be known as the Blitz, and London's East End bore the main brunt of the bombs.

In early September 1940, Buckingham Palace was also bombed. In describing what happened, Queen Elizabeth wrote to Queen Mary of the "horrible attack" and how she saw "a great column of smoke & earth thrown up into the air" and of a "tremendous explosion." More bombs fell later on, inflicting serious damage to Buckingham Palace and sending the King and Queen's nerves on edge. The first bombing of Buckingham Palace had prompted a shaken Queen Elizabeth to make her famous remark, "I'm glad we've been bombed. It makes feel I can look the East End in the face."

With war raging, and bombs raining on London and casualties mounting, it was decided that Lilibet should make a speech to be broadcast on the radio in order to help rally the spirits of the children of Britain and the Empire. In October, Princess Elizabeth spoke in high-pitched, encouraging voice to the children in a speech in which she said that, "in the end all will be well." Then, turning to her sister, sitting next to her, Elizabeth added, "we are both going to say good night to you. Come on, Margaret." The ten-year-old Princess spoke up and said, "Good night and good luck to you all."

Many children and adults heard this special broadcast on their radios. In her speech, Lilibet sounded younger than she was. But the fourteen-year-old Princess spoke clearly and with resolve, giving strength and confidence to countless people, for "in that lone, touching voice, amid the ongoing catastrophe of war, lay the hope of Britain."

Any comfort and hope Princess Elizabeth and the royal family could offer was needed and appreciated. Since September 1940, Nazi Germany had been relentless in bombing the British capital. In January 1941, the Queen wrote to her mother-in-law of her anger at what London had to suffer during the Blitz, saying how "enraged beyond <u>words</u>" she was "over the futile and wicked destruction of the City of

London." With all the bombing and destruction around London, it came as no surprise that the King and Queen relished their weekends at Windsor Castle where they were reunited with their growing daughters.

In the summer of 1941, a series of photographs was taken of the Queen with her two daughters on the grounds of Windsor Castle. They were idyllic photographs: Queen Elizabeth in a printed summer dress with hat and pearls. The Princesses, dressed alike in pastel pink, even though by now, Lilibet was fifteen and as tall as her mother. Princess Elizabeth by this time, continued to be a dutiful and serious girl, while Princess Margaret was by far, the more flamboyant and mischievous of the two. Lady Airlie, one of Queen Mary's confidantes, had expressed her opinion about the girls' personalities, dubbing Princess Elizabeth as "one of the most unselfish girls I have ever met." Queen Mary, on Margaret, found her to be "*espiègle*," saying, "all the same, she is so outrageously amusing that one can't help encouraging her." Margaret, however outgoing and amusing, was not the one destined for the throne; Elizabeth was.

Naturally, the question of who Elizabeth might marry materialized during the war years as she matured. There were the occasional aristocrats who visited who were thought to be possible suitors, but by this time, Lilibet's mind had been made up. She had eyes only for Prince Philip of Greece, who served in the Royal Navy. They occasionally corresponded; and Elizabeth was daring enough to show her devotion by having a framed photograph of the handsome prince in her sitting room.

At Windsor, the two sisters performed in pantomimes along with local school children, the monies raised going to the Queen's charities. The first pantomime, *Cinderella*, was performed in Christmas of 1941. Princess Margaret's artistic personality shone through during the performances. But it was Princess Elizabeth who surprised those who watched her as she sang, acted, and danced on stage, showing a vivacity and verve that had been hidden behind her normal, quiet reserve. This first pantomime was followed by others, including *Aladdin* in 1943 and *Old Mother Red Riding Boots* in 1944. Prince Philip had attended the *Aladdin* pantomime and watched in the front row in amusement as a vivacious Princess Elizabeth, joked, sang, and danced her way through the performance. Crawfie noticed how animated Lilibet was, recalling in her memoirs that: "There was a sparkle about her none of us had ever seen before. Many people remarked on it."

The pantomimes helped to divert Princess Elizabeth's concerns over the war, including worries about Prince Philip, who was in active service in Britain's Royal Navy. In 1941, Prince Philip, went on shore leave and visited Elizabeth and her parents at Windsor Castle. The idea of Philip marrying Lilibet had already been floated about. It was the great ambition of his uncle and mentor, Lord Mountbatten, to see the youngsters married one day, but in 1941, they were much too young at fifteen and twenty-one to contemplate it seriously.

In March 1942, Princess Elizabeth was confirmed at Windsor by the Archbishop of Canterbury in "a simple little service" as the Queen described it. Of the Princess, the Archbishop concluded that, "though naturally not very communicative, she showed real intelligence and understanding." Lady Airlie, who moved in court circles since the Victorian era, noted that, "the carriage of her head was unequalled, and there was about her that indescribable something which Queen Victoria had."

A month after she was confirmed, Princess Elizabeth turned sixteen and was appointed Colonel of the Grenadier Guards. By this time, the Princess had grown into an attractive young lady with bright blue eyes, dark brown hair, a good figure, and a clear, flawless complexion. Turning sixteen also meant that Elizabeth began to partake in more public duties. King George VI also began to prepare his elder daughter in the craft of kingship by explaining the fine points of being a monarch. This same year, Antoinette de Bellaigue joined the Princesses at Windsor to help them perfect their French. De Bellaigue recalled Princess Elizabeth as having "had an instinct for the right thing. She was her simple self, *très naturelle*. And there was always a strong sense of duty mixed with *joie de vivre* in the pattern of her character."

War continued to rage and in August of 1942, tragedy struck the royal family when Elizabeth's paternal uncle, the Duke of Kent, was killed when the RAF plane he was on bound for Iceland, crashed in Scotland, leaving his wife, Marina, a widow with three young children. That such a tragedy could happen to her Aunt Marina, would likely have made Princess Elizabeth think of the dangers Prince Philip of Greece faced in the theater of war. Prince Philip saw action during the war, being mentioned in despatches for meritorious service in face of the enemy during the Battle of Matapan in 1941. In 1942, he was promoted to Lieutenant. Though he fought on the British side, Philip was still a Prince of Greece at this time. Though there had been talk that

Philip might become a naturalized British subject, it was not pursued. King George VI explained to Lord Mountbatten that this was not the right moment for Philip to become a British subject because his brothers-in-law had ties with Nazi Germany. This plus the turbulent Greek political situation, made it difficult for Philip, a foreign royal, to obtain British citizenship was at the time.

Already at this time, there was speculation that Prince Philip might be a possible husband for Princess Elizabeth. Already at this time, there was speculation that Prince Philip might be a possible husband for Princess Elizabeth. The diarist, Chips Channon, recorded meeting the "extraordinarily handsome" Prince in Athens in 1941. Channon noted in his diary a conversation he had with Princess Nicholas of Greece, the mother of the Duchess of Kent, in which Channon learned of Philip's possible future: "He is to be our Prince Consort, and that is why he is serving on our Navy."

In 1944, Prince Philip visited the royal family at their home, Balmoral, in Scotland. Queen Mary became convinced that it was from this year that Philip and Lilibet's affection for each other grew. Queen Mary confided to her friend, Lady Airlie, that the young couple "have been in love for the last eighteen months. In fact longer, I think. I believe she fell in love with him the first time he went down to Windsor, but the King and Queen feel that she is too young to be engaged yet. They want her to see more of the world before committing herself, and to meet more men. After all, she's only nineteen, and one is very impressionable at that age." Philip's cousin, King George II of Greece, had written to King George VI, requesting that Philip be considered as a suitor for Elizabeth's hand, but George VI replied that his daughter was too young.

When Princess Elizabeth turned eighteen, she was made a Counsellor of State. The milestone birthday celebrations were kept relatively quiet and included a luncheon with family including Queen Mary; Princess Marina; the Duke and Duchess of Gloucester; and the Princess Royal and her husband, the Earl of Harewood. In writing to Lady Desborough about it, Elizabeth said: "My eighteenth birthday was a very busy one, and I spent it amongst the family, and a great many Grenadiers and old friends."

When she turned eighteen, Princess Elizabeth also took on some high-profile public engagements that took her away from Windsor. Having spent four years living at Windsor Castle, the Princess had come to appreciate the castle compound. Queen Elizabeth admitted as much to

Queen Mary, telling her that, "I am glad to say that Lilibet has also a great affection and admiration for the whole place…" Princess Elizabeth's more public profile raised people's awareness of her and the overwhelming impression was a positive one, so that "she found herself an emblematic heroine everywhere. All over the Empire, the health, beauty and emerging womanhood of the Princess were linked to the eagerly anticipated future, in which families would be brought together, sweethearts rejoined, babies born, bellies filled and freedom enjoyed."

In 1945, Elizabeth was allowed to join the Auxiliary Territorial Service (ATS) and was given the honorary rank of second subaltern. In a letter to Queen Mary, Queen Elizabeth explained that Lilibet was "going to do a course in mechanics with the ATS … I think it will be a good thing for her to have a little experience from the inside into how a women's Service is run. She will learn something about the inside of a car, which is always useful." The letter did not disclose that by letting Elizabeth pursue this mechanics course, her parents had hoped that she would pine less for Prince Philip as well. There was no chance of that. By this time, Princess Elizabeth was certain that Philip was the only one she would consider as a future husband.

At the end of her weeks-long ATS course, Elizabeth knew the basics of rebuilding truck engines and could drive ambulances and change their wheels. The Princess's ATS course was the last formal training Elizabeth undertook. The education she received from Crawfie and Henry Marten, along with the polishing of her French from Antoinette de Bellaigue meant that Princess Elizabeth's formal education was complete. Added to this was the Princess's increasing interest and knowledge about horses and horse breeding. Other sporting enthusiasms including stalking deer in the royal family's Scottish estate of Balmoral, an enthusiasm Elizabeth shared with her father.

Princess Elizabeth had become King George VI's "trusty squire" while Princess Margaret with her "jokes, japes, and mischief" had become the King's "jester." As time passed, Princess Elizabeth continued to remain grounded and dutiful while Princess Margaret developed "an uneasy blend of grandiosity and rebellion." And as "the younger [sister] became more wilful and wayward, making the most of her privileged status, the elder became more withdrawn, worried about her destiny – and perhaps even guilty about it." Despite the disparate personalities of the sisters, Elizabeth's "unusually lovely nature," as Crawfie put it, eased the friction that could have easily marred the sisters' relationship. "All her feeling for her pretty little sister," recalled Crawfie, "was motherly and protective."

At nineteen, Princess Elizabeth had emerged from the shadow of the war and the nursery, a dutiful young woman much like her father. Elizabeth was "unlike her mother, always the life and soul of parties," nor was the Princess anything like "her sparkling younger sister." Princess Elizabeth, recalled a friend of the era, "was a shy girl who didn't find social life easy" and consequently did not find herself at ease in parties. But such drawbacks were minor and did not bother the Princess whose thoughts by this time were dominated by a future with Prince Philip. "She was a stunning girl," recalled a friend of Elizabeth at the time, "longing to be a young wife without too many problems."

On May 8, 1945, celebrations broke out in London with Victory in Europe Day. The war had ended at last after nearly six years of fighting. Dense crowds of jubilant Londoners cheering themselves hoarse flocked in front of Buckingham Palace where King George VI, Queen Elizabeth, Winston Churchill, and the Princesses Elizabeth and Margaret stood on the balcony, waving and acknowledging the cheers. For many, seeing the two Princesses that day was a revelation. When the war began, Elizabeth and Margaret were just thirteen and nine years of age. In May 1945, Elizabeth was twenty and Margaret almost fifteen, and both had grown into attractive youth women.

With the excitement of VE Day unfolding before them, the sisters begged their parents to let them celebrate with the crowds outside the palace. The King and Queen agreed. Elizabeth, in her ATS uniform, along with Margaret, and a small group mingled with the crowds, chanting like the others, asking for the King and Queen. The sisters were swept up by the joy exuded by the crowds around them and cheered their parents who appeared on the palace balcony again to acknowledge their subjects. The war had kept Elizabeth and Margaret isolated and given them little chance of seeing much of the world outside of Windsor Castle. King George VI understood this, prompting him to say: "Poor darlings, they have never had any fun yet."

Chapter 9. Victoria: Accession

When seventeen-year-old Prince Albert of Saxe-Coburg-Gotha and his older brother, Prince Ernst, visited England in May 1836, they made an impression on Princess Victoria whom she referred to as 'Dearest Albert' and 'Dearest Ernst.' She noted that Albert had the same blue eyes as she did and the same light brown hair color. Both brothers liked art and drew and played the piano. Both were clever, "particularly Albert." Victoria admitted in admiration that "the charm of his countenance is his expression, which is most delightful; *c'est à la fois* full of goodness and sweetness, and very clever and intelligent."

Prince Albert, in turn, found Victoria to have been "very amiable" and self-possessed. The Prince left England in a favorable light, which pleased King Leopold. By this time, Victoria had learned of her uncle's marital plans for her and Albert and as the King's wishes "were law to her," the Princess wrote to King Leopold: "I hope and trust that all will go on prosperously and well on this subject, now of so much importance to me." The manner in which

Princess Victoria described Prince Albert to King Leopold could not have pleased the King more when she wrote in June 1836:

> *I must thank you my beloved Uncle, for the prospect of great happiness you have contributed* [sic] *to give me, in the person of Dear Albert. Allow me then, my dearest Uncle, to tell you how delighted I am with him, and how much I like him in every way. He possesses every quality that could be desired to make me perfectly happy. He is so sensible, so kind and so good and amiable too. He has besides the most pleasing and delightful exterior and appearance that you could wish to see.*

Once Prince Albert and Prince Ernst's visit was over, Princess Victoria returned to her uneasy life at Kensington Palace. Relations between the Princess and Sir John Conroy did not improve; the same could be said for the Duchess of Kent and King William. In fact, their relationship had deteriorated to the extent that it caused a scandal in August 1836. An incident involving King William IV and the

Duchess of Kent exploded, shocking numerous individuals, including Princess Victoria.

The Princess and the Duchess of Kent had been invited to stay with the King and Queen for a week at Windsor to celebrate King William and Queen Adelaide's birthdays. The Duchess, however, chose to stay only one night. This annoyed the King. His anger had already been stoked when he heard that the Duchess had occupied a suite of seventeen rooms in Kensington Palace which he had not allowed her. When the King greeted Princess Victoria at Windsor Castle, he took both her hands and told her how pleased he was to see her and regretted that they had not met more often. Then, turning to the Duchess of Kent, King William upbraided her for taking over the suite of rooms at Kensington Palace despite his orders. In front of numerous guests, King William said that, "he neither understood nor would endure conduct so disrespectful to him."

Even more shocking was the King's outburst at his birthday dinner where a hundred guests attended. Next to King William sat the Duchess of Kent and opposite the King sat Princess Victoria. After the King's health was drunk, he broke out in a tirade that mortified everyone present, saying in a loud voice and excited manner:

I trust in God that my life may be spared for nine months longer, after which period, in the event of my death, no regency would take place. I should then have the satisfaction of leaving the royal authority to the personal exercise of that young lady (pointing to the Princess), the heiress presumptive of the Crown, and not in the hands of a person now near me, who is surrounded by evil advisers and who is herself incompetent to act with propriety in the station in which she would be placed ... Amongst many other things I have particularly to complain of the manner in which that young lady has been kept away from my Court; she has been repeatedly kept from my drawing-rooms, at which she ought always to have been present, but I am fully resolved that this shall not happen again. I would have her know that I am King and I determined to make my authority respected, and for the future, I shall insist and command that the Princess do upon all

occasions appear at my Court, as it is
her duty to do.

When the King ended his tirade, Queen Adelaide looked shocked, Princess Victoria burst into tears, and the Duchess of Kent sat in stony silence. King William IV had made his point in spectacular fashion. The King's denunciation of his sister-in-law was so forceful and shocking that it caused a permanent rupture between them. There was no turning back. King William IV and the Duchess of Kent were mortal enemies – and Princess Victoria was right in the middle of the warring royals.

The early months of 1837 King William still alive. Victoria was still a gilded prisoner of Kensington Palace where "she was being kept close, Conroy and the Duchess did not intend to let her escape from their grasp during this critical period." With King William IV's health declining, Sir John Conroy became as anxious as ever to secure his power when it came to the future Queen Victoria. As her eighteenth birthday in May neared, Conroy, who had been as anxious as ever to entrench himself as Victoria's indispensable secretary and become the power behind the throne, became agitated. Baron Stockmar, who was in London and saw what was happening, wrote to King Leopold, reporting that Conroy told him that even if Victoria succeeded to the throne at 18 and no regency was needed, she was still legally a minor and therefore subject to control until she turned 21. "God knows," Stockmar told Leopold, "what schemes are being built on this fact…"

More disagreements involving the Duchess of Kent and King William occurred over the King's offer of an income and separate establishment to Princess Victoria. This enraged the Duchess because it would mean separation between her and Victoria – something the Duchess could not countenance. The isolated Princess was compelled to sign a letter saying that she was to remain as she was, in effect tethered to her mother. When King William read his niece's missive, he noted angrily that, "Victoria has not written that letter." The Princess may have been compelled to sign the letter but there was little doubt that she possessed an obstinate streak.

The Duchess of Kent was exasperated with Victoria's willfulness and told her daughter, "you are still very young" and that "all your success so far has been due to your *Mother's* reputation. Do not be *too sanguine* in your own *talents* and *understanding*."

During this time, feelers were sent by the British Minister in Berlin, Lord William Russell, that Prince Adalbert of Prussia, wished to visit Princess Victoria with the idea that he might present himself as a suitor for her hand in marriage. The Duchess of Kent wrote back, saying that, "I could not, compatibly with those I owe my child, the King, and the country, give your Lordship the answer you desire; the application should go to the King. But if I know my duty to the King, I know also my maternal ones, and I will candidly tell your Lordship that I am of [the] opinion that the Princess should not marry till she is much older. I will also add that, in the choice of person to share her great destiny, I have but one wish – that her happiness and the interest of the country be realised in it."

On May 24, 1837, the momentous day arrived in which Princess Victoria reached her eighteenth birthday. London celebrated with brightly illuminated streets and "crowds of eager spectators" as *The Times* recorded, "rendered the streets impassable." King William gave a ball in her honor. As for Victoria, she wrote in her journal: "How old! and yet how far am I from being what I should be." She vowed that "I shall from this day take the *firm* resolution to study … to keep my attention always well fixed on whatever I am about, and to strive every day to become less trifling and more fit for what, if Heaven wills it, I'm some day to be!"

With Victoria attaining her majority, the need for a regency was gone. Conroy was exasperated. Everything he had worked hard for, everything he had hoped for, was slipping away. With Victoria's attainment of her majority and the need for a regency gone, Conroy made one last gamble. He demanded that the Princess appoint him as her private secretary. Victoria refused.

As King William's health failed, Victoria's ascension to the throne was imminent. And because this was so, there were fears of the "schemes and intrigues of those who would exert all their power to entrap the most isolated young Princess, hoping thus to rule the future Sovereign." Baron Stockmar was in London at King Leopold's behest to ensure that that "the compass," i.e., Victoria's constant stream advice from King Leopold should not be ignored by the Princess. Stockmar also tried to mitigate Princess Victoria's situation. He supported her as did Baroness Lehzen in her battle against Conroy.

On June 9th, King William's condition worsened. Baron Stockmar had a long talk with Princess Victoria that day and found her "cool and collected, and her answers precise, apt and determined." Stockmar concluded that Victoria was "not at all inclined to do anything which would put Conroy into a situation to be able to entrench upon them [i.e., her rights and future power]. Her feelings seem, moreover, to have been deeply wounded by what she calls 'his impudent and insulting conduct' towards her."

Sir John Conroy, in desperation pressed the Duchess of Kent to put pressure on Princess Victoria in mid-June and declared that "if Princess Victoria will not listen to reason, *she must be coerced*." But Conroy abandoned this last desperate act only because, he admitted, the Duchess of Kent, he thought, could not be relied upon to take such a drastic step.

By June 19, it was clear that King William was slipping away, and when Princess Victoria was told this she burst into tears. In the very early morning of June 20, 1837, King William IV died at Windsor Castle at the age of seventy-one. Upon his death, "the last barrier between Princess Victoria and the crown was thus removed."

The task of breaking the news of King William's death to Victoria fell upon the late King's chamberlain, Lord Conyngham, and the Archbishop of Canterbury. They raced to London from Windsor and arrived at Kensington Palace "in the gray of the early dawn." The two men found the inhabitants of the palace still deep in slumber. There were delays in gaining entrance and the duo made several frantic attempts at ringing bells in order to be admitted in. When a sleepy servant greeted them, Conyngham and the Archbishop demanded an audience with Victoria on "very important business." When the men were told that Princess Victoria was still asleep, the Archbishop replied: "We are come on business of State, to *the Queen*, and even her sleep must give way."

The Duchess of Kent awoke Victoria at six in the morning. She placed a shawl over her plain nightgown, put on her slippers and went downstairs to meet the two men alone. Lord Conyngham and the Archbishop knelt before the petite young woman before them and told them of her uncle's death. Both men were thus the first of Queen Victoria's subjects to pay her homage. Victoria was Queen of the United Kingdom of Great Britain and Ireland, and the colonies. When the Archbishop of Canterbury, upon informing the young Victoria what her first request as monarch was, she replied, "I ask your prayers on my behalf."

Upon meeting her mother again, Victoria burst into tears. She felt sorrow for her uncle's death and also the burden of being thrust into the position of Queen Regnant. It did not take long, however, for

Victoria to appreciate her newly independent position. That same day, the new Queen ordered that her bed be removed from her mother's room. Victoria also received her Prime Minister, Lord Melbourne, alone.

Next, came Queen Victoria's first Privy Council meeting, consisting of former and current members of Parliament whose task it was to advise their monarch. Dressed plainly in black, the young Queen impressed the room of men with her demeanor; and in spite of her youth and inexperience, exuded a sense of gravitas. One witness was impressed with the young monarch, noting that he was "amazed … at her manner and behavior, at her apparent deep sense of her situation, her modesty, and at the same time her firmness. She appeared, in fact, to be awed, but not daunted…" The Duke of Wellington, vanquisher of Napoleon in the Battle of Waterloo, was also a witness and remarked, "if she had been his own daughter he could not have desired to see her perform her part better."

Another witness noted Victoria's "self-possession" and that "her voice, which is naturally beautiful, was clear and untroubled, and her eye was bright and calm, neither bold nor downcast, but firm and soft. There was a blush on her cheek which made her look both handsomer and more interesting; and certainly she did look as interesting and handsome as any young lady I ever saw."

The conclusion of those who watched Queen Victoria at her first Privy Council meeting mirrored that of the diarist Charles Greville who was present: "The young Queen ... behaves with a decorum and propriety beyond her years, and with all the sedateness and dignity the want of which was so conspicuous in her uncle [King William IV]."

The Victorian era had begun. It was the age of Pax Britannica where the Royal Navy ruled the seas and Britain's industrial supremacy was the envy of the world. The British Empire grew unmatched in history, covering nearly one-fourth of the world's surface. Over this great flourishing of domestic and imperial achievement reigned Queen Victoria.

The Victorian era ended with Queen Victoria's death in 1901, after a long reign of nearly sixty-four years, surpassed in length by her great-great-granddaughter, Queen Elizabeth II, in 2015.

Chapter 10. Elizabeth: Accession

In the summer of 1946, a momentous event took place in the life of Princess Elizabeth. Prince Philip visited the royal family in Balmoral and proposed to the twenty-year-old Princess, who accepted. Elizabeth described the engagement as having taken place "beside some well-loved loch, the white clouds sailing over-head and a curlew crying just out of sight…" The King and Queen had accepted Philip as a potential son-in-law, though Queen Elizabeth found "the briskness of her prospective son-in-law slightly unappealing." King George VI had not objected to the couple's engagement, though he stipulated that a final decision and announcement should be made only after the royal family returned from an official visit to South Africa in early 1947. King George's opposition to Elizabeth becoming quickly engaged to Philip stemmed not so much on possessiveness on the King's part but "it was simply that, having suffered so bleak a youth himself, the King was anxious to prolong this period of idyllic family happiness. With a wife whom he adored and two daughters to whom he was devoted, King George VI can be forgiven for wanting to keep this unit intact for as long as possible."

There were courtiers who objected to Prince Philip as a future consort and thought that Princess Elizabeth could have done better. "There was no single, or over-riding objection," wrote a biographer of Elizabeth's on the topic, "just the raised eyebrow, the closing of ranks at which royalty and the landed classes were peculiarly adept. If there was a unifying theme, it was a kind of jealous, chauvinistic protectiveness – based on a belief that so precious an asset [as Princess Elizabeth] could not be lightly handed over, least of all to the penniless scion of a disreputable house who, in the nostrils of his critics, had about him the whiff of a fortune-hunter." Princess Elizabeth brushed aside all the niggling objections as her mind had been made up on Philip as her future husband. There was no doubt that "the self-reliance bred in him by his difficult upbringing could come across as cockiness, and he could appear arrogant when brushing aside obstacles in order to get things done. However, his forthrightness and independence were precisely the traits that had won Elizabeth's heart, accustomed as she had been all her life to fawning deference."

In January 1947, Princess Elizabeth dutifully accompanied her parents and Princess Margaret on a tour of South Africa. They left a bitterly cold London and boarded the H.M.S. *Vanguard* for the long journey. In Cape Town, in April, the Princess turned twenty-one and came of age. From there, she broadcast a speech to the Empire in which Princess Elizabeth made a solemn act of dedication to her future subjects. In her high-pitched cultured voice, Elizabeth announced that, "I declare before you all that my whole life, whether it be long or short, shall be devoted to your service ... God help me to make good my vows and God bless you all who are willing to share in it." Back in England, Clement Attlee, the Prime Minister, paid tribute to the future Queen, acknowledging that the Princess had "lived though some of the hardest yet noblest years of these islands' long history" and spoke of Elizabeth's "simple dignity and wise understanding."

The trip to South Africa had not deterred Princess Elizabeth from her desire to marry Prince Philip. "As it was with her horses – and her dogs, and her faith, and her duty – so it was with Philip." In July 1947 the couple's engagement was formally announced. By that time, Princess Elizabeth's fiancé had become a British subject and taken his mother's surname, becoming Lieutenant Philip Mountbatten.

In a letter to Philip, Queen Elizabeth wrote of her feelings and those of the King, saying: "how happy we feel about this engagement and to say how glad we are to have you as a son-in-law … I know that we can trust our darling Lilibet to your love and care … & am certain that you will be a great help & comfort to our very beloved little daughter." The engagement also pleased Queen Mary who wrote in her diary: "Heard with great pleasure of darling Lilibet's engagement to Philip Mountbatten. They both came to see me after luncheon looking radiant." And as for the Countess of Airlie, Queen Mary's old friend, she too, had her marked opinions, especially on Philip's potential impact on Elizabeth: "Observing him I thought that he had far more character than most people would imagine. I wondered whether he would be capable of helping Princess Elizabeth some day as the Prince Consort had helped Queen Victoria." The Countess also noted of the future bride: "When I looked at Princess Elizabeth, flushed and radiant with happiness, I was again reminded of Queen Victoria. Although the Queen had been old, plain and fat when I had seen her and this girl was young, pretty and slim she had the same air of majesty."

As a future consort to the Heiress Presumptive, King George VI deemed it right that his future son-in-law be granted appropriate rank and titles. The King thus bestowed upon Philip the style of 'Royal Highness' as well as the titles, Duke of Edinburgh, Earl of Merioneth, and Baron Greenwich.

The wedding took place on November 20, 1947; and "in grey, war-wracked Britain, the wedding seemed like herald of better times; almost like a reaffirmation of Britain's place in the world." Indeed, the wedding took place amidst a time of austere conditions when "victorious Britain seemed to be on her knees."

On the morning of the wedding, Crawfie visited the bride in her room, looking out the window at the excited crowds gathered in front of Buckingham Palace.

"I can't believe it's really happening, Crawfie," said Elizabeth to her former governess. "I have to keep pinching myself."

The bride's gown was a lovely confection in ivory silk satin embroidered with raised pearls with a 15-foot train. Designed by Norman Hartnell, the gown would not have been possible had the Princess not been allowed extra ration coupons for her wedding dress. A number of the Princess's future subjects had been generous, too, in helping out with the dress by sending their coupons. The splendor of the wedding, held at Westminster Abbey, provided a splash of color and pageantry which had not been seen since the years before the war. But for all its splendid ceremonial, the wedding was, above all, a family affair. Queen Alexandra of Yugoslavia, Philip's cousin, was present and recalled that, "one wanted to cry at this wedding. The age-old ritual caught at the heart." King George VI, in a moving letter to his daughter, wrote of his own strong sentiments, saying that, "I was so proud of you and thrilled at having you so close to me on our long walk in Westminster Abbey, but when I handed your hand to the Archbishop I felt I had lost something very precious." The King, though, added a more positive note, saying that, "I can, I know, always count on you, and now Philip, to help us in our work."

Four days after the wedding, Queen Elizabeth, in reply to a letter her newly married daughter had written to her parents, wrote back in reply: "Darling Lilibet, no parents ever had a better daughter, you are always such an unselfish & thoughtful angel to Papa & me, & we are so thankful for all your goodness and sweetness … That you & Philip should be blissfully happy & love each other through good days and bad or depressing days is my one wish …"

Philip, in turn, wrote a moving letter to his mother-in-law about his devotion to his new wife: "Lilibet is the only 'thing' in this world which is absolutely real to me and my ambition is to weld the two of us into a new combined existence that will not only be able to withstand the shocks directed at us but will also have a positive existence for the good … very humbly, I thank God for Lilibet and for us."

Elizabeth and Philip's happiness was augmented in November 1948 when the Princess gave birth to Prince Charles. In Early 1949, Queen Elizabeth wrote of her first grandchild, saying that, "the baby is so sweet, & Lilibet & Philip are enchanted, and we are so happy for them." The family's happiness was blighted, however, by concerns over the health of King George VI. Arteriosclerosis had set in and years of heavy smoking, along with the strain and stress of the war had all taken their toll on the King. Under doctors' advice, the King canceled a planned tour of Australia and New Zealand.

In the meantime, in post-war Britain, the desire for decolonization picked up speed and the break-up of the British Empire began in earnest. In August 1947, India, under its last Viceroy, Lord Louis Mountbatten, became independent. The King ceased being Emperor of India and upon Elizabeth's accession, she would not be styled Empress of India like her great-great-grandmother, Queen Victoria.

Unlike Victoria, who was thrust into the role of queen at eighteen, Elizabeth had the good fortune of enjoying some tranquil years with Prince Philip and their growing family. They had a home to call their own in London: Clarence House, not far from Buckingham Palace. And in late 1949, Elizabeth joined her husband in Malta where he was stationed with the Royal Navy. This was the start of two periods away from England for Elizabeth (who left Prince Charles with the King and Queen), providing her with the closest semblance of normal life.

In August 1950, Princess Elizabeth gave birth to a daughter, Princess Anne, in London. From November 1950 to February 1951, and then again from March to April of that year, Elizabeth joined Philip in Malta again, this time leaving Charles and Anne with their maternal grandparents. But with the King's health declining, this Maltese idyll did not last. In 1951, concerns for George VI's health increased. In September 1951, George VI's left lung was removed, damaged from years of heavy smoking; unbeknownst to the King, he was suffering from cancer. All this meant that Elizabeth and Philip undertook more engagements. In October 1951, the couple embarked on an official tour of Canada, crisscrossing the vast country. Elizabeth and Philip were cheered and welcomed everywhere they went. This successful Canadian tour was soon followed by another one to Australia and New Zealand. On January 31, 1952, Elizabeth and Philip left a cold, wintry London, headed for the first leg of their tour, East Africa. Queen Elizabeth, Princess Margaret, and King George VI were at Heathrow airport to see them off. The King, looking frail, bid his daughter and son-in-law good-bye, saying, "look out for yourselves."

At the beginning of February, the King and Queen, along with Princess Margaret, and Prince Charles and Princess Anne left for Sandringham, the royal estate in Norfolk. On the early morning of February 6th, King George VI died in his sleep, aged 56. When told of the death of the King, the Prime Minister, Winston Churchill, teary-eyed, told his secretary, Jock Colville, of the new Queen, that "he did not know her and that she was only a child."

In a letter to the late King's mother, Queen Mary, Queen Elizabeth wrote of her shock and sorrow: "It is hard to grasp, he was such an angel to the children & me, and I cannot bear to think of Lilibet, so young to bear such a burden."

At the time of her father's death, Elizabeth was faraway in Kenya. She and Philip had gone to

Treetops, a lodge built high up a huge fig tree in the jungle. They watched before them under bright stars and a glimmering moon, elephants trumpeting, warthogs grunting, bulls fighting, and a herd of rhinoceros stealthily passing by. Elizabeth and Philip retired for the night and then left the next morning for Sagana Lodge. It was there that Philip learned from Elizabeth's private secretary of the death of King George VI. Philip broke the news to his wife; and some of their retinue recalled how the couple walked alone in the garden. Philip's own private secretary noted how he saw Elizabeth "weeping desperately for the loss of her father" but afterwards "straightened up" and returned to the lodge where she was asked by her secretary, Martin Charteris, by what regnal name she wished to be called. "My own name, of course," she replied, "Elizabeth." And upon seeing her lady-in-waiting, Pamela Mountbatten Hicks (daughter of Lord Mountbatten), the new Queen apologized: "Oh, I'm so sorry, it means we've all got to go home, I'm afraid."

After a long twenty-four-hour flight, the new Queen Elizabeth II arrived back at Heathrow, where only a week before, she had bid farewell to her father. To Pamela Hicks, their arrival in London meant that for the Queen, "the end of her private life had come." Composed and dressed in black mourning, Queen Elizabeth II descended the plane's steps and greeted the awaiting dignitaries, among them her Prime Minister, Winston Churchill; the Duke of Gloucester; and Lord Mountbatten.

At Clarence House, Queen Elizabeth received a special visitor, Queen Mary. "Her old Grannie and subject," noted Queen Mary, who had just lost her third son, "must be the first to kiss her hand." And so it was. At Clarence House, in the late afternoon, "Queen Mary was received by her eldest granddaughter, who at the early age of twenty-five was thus suddenly invested with the mystic aura of the British Crown."

The funeral of King George VI took place on February 15, 1952. Among those in attendance were the late King's daughter, widow, and mother - three Queens dressed in deepest black, their faces obscured by their long veils. Upon burying her beloved father, Queen Elizabeth II also saw the burial of a beloved monarch. The scepter – and burden of monarchy - had been passed to her. In her message to the nation, the newly widowed Queen Elizabeth said, "I commend to you our dear Daughter: give her your loyalty and devotion: though blessed with a husband and children she will need your protection and your love in the great and lonely station to which she has been called."

Did you enjoy this book?

I hope you enjoyed reading this book. If you did, I would be most grateful if you could please post a brief review on Amazon.

Please see my other books on the Royal Cavalcade series as well. I hope you will find another book or several books from the series which you may come to enjoy. I welcome hearing from my readers. You may reach me via my website at: www.juliapgelardi.com.

<u>ENDNOTES</u>

<u>Introduction</u>

"she is completely …. of her presence…": Elizabeth Longford, *The Queen: The Life of Elizabeth II* (New York: Alfred A. Knopf, 1983), p. 15.

<u>Chapter 1</u>

"was a tall …. charming and attractive.": Baron E. von Stockmar, *Memoirs of Baron Stockmar*. Edited by F. Max Müller (London: Longmans, Green, and Co., 1873), pp. 75-7.

"The greatest and …. in her own country.": Richard Hough, *Victoria and Albert* (New York: St. Martin's Press, 1996), p. 1.

"plump as a partridge": Stockmar, *Memoirs*, p. 78.

"which was destined …. the English nation": Mary F. Sandars, *The Life and Times of Queen Adelaide* (London: Stanley Paul & Co., 1915), p. 63.

"she will be Queen of England.": Stockmar, *Memoirs*, p. 78.

"I cannot find …. English like Queens.": Hough, *Victoria and Albert*, p. 6.

"let her be …. with tempestuous sobs.": Elizabeth Longford, *Queen Victoria: Born to Succeed* (New York: Harper & Row, Publishers, 1964), pp. 23-4.

"was born into …. in grave doubt.": Hough, *Victoria and Albert*, p. 1.

"she held her …. as though delighted.": Sandars, *Queen Adelaide*, p. 83.

"Uncle William and …. many, many others.": *Ibid.*, pp. 90-1.

"friendless and alone …. not her own.": Sidney Lee, *Queen Victoria: A Biography* (London: John Murray, 1904), p. 61.

"I was always …. a soldier's child.": Lee, *Queen Victoria*, p. 17.

"I am already …. will think wise!": Lynn Vallone, *Becoming Victoria* (New Haven, CT: Yale University Press, 2001), p. 20.

"beginning to show …. own little way.": *Ibid.*, p. 19.

"She knew me …. but for me.": Lee, *Queen Victoria*, p. 20.

Chapter 2

"there would be …. a social revolution.": Carolly Erickson, *Lilibet: An Intimate Portrait of Elizabeth II* (New York: St. Martin's Press, 2004), p. 4.

"worried about his .... nerves with drink.": *Ibid.*, p. 5.

"her children were .... destroyed her character.": Hector Bolitho, *King George VI* (Philadelphia: J.B. Lippincott Company, 1939), pp.162-3.

"You don't know .... so wonderful & strange.": William Shawcross, ed.,*Counting One's Blessings: The Selected Letters of Queen Elizabeth the Queen Mother* (New York: Farrar, Straus and Giroux, 2012), p. 147.

"She is perfectly .... all love her.": Lady Cynthia Asquith, *Her Majesty the Queen: An Entirely New and Complete Biography* (New York: E.P. Dutton & Company, 1937), p. 141.

"being incapable of .... gentle and disarming.": *Ibid.*, p. 88.

"a striving for .... intelligence and acumen.": *Ibid.*, p. 101.

"Pink-skinned and .... Longford, *The Queen*, p. 30.

"She was a .... the Prince of Wales.": Jennifer Ellis, ed., *Thatched with Gold: The Memoirs of Mabell, Countess of Airlie* (London: Hutchinson of London, 1962), p. 179.

"It was the .... like a tantrum.": Robert Lacey, *Monarch: The Life and Reign of Elizabeth II* (New York: Free Press, 2002), p. 80.

"I hardly think that necessary.": *Ibid.*

"your family …. pretty.": Longford, *The Queen*, p. 30.

"The possibility that …. its Royal destiny.": Shawcross, *Counting One's Blessings*, p. 75.

"A possible Queen …. a possible Queen-Empress.": Lacey, *Monarch*, p. 78.

"From the beginning …. by the public.": Bolitho, *King George VI*, p. 174.

"Upward of three …. to a halt.": Erickson, *Lilibet*, p. 9.

"very miserable at …. doesn't realize anything.": 6 January 1927 diary entry, Shawcross, *Counting One's Blessings*, p. 151.

"the baby was …. broke me up!": 9 January 1927, the Duchess of York to Queen Mary, *Ibid.*, p. 151.

"I am looking …. see her again.": 12 June 1927, the Duchess of York to King George V, *Ibid.*, p. 161.

"a little darling": Longford, *The Queen*, p. 30.

"brilliant blue gaze …. by importunate admirers…": Asquith, *Her Majesty*, p. 136.

"G. delighted to …. & so sympathetic." James Pope-Hennessy, *Queen Mary, 1867-1953* (London: George Allen and Unwin, Ltd., 1959), p. 546.

"Queen Victoria's earliest …. a nice archbishop.": Longford, *The Queen*, p. 36.

"always came first .... bearable to him": Ellis, *Thatched with Gold*, p. 180.

"boomed like the .... at Buckingham Palace.": Longford, *The Queen*, pp. 36-7.

"never forgot the .... exactly the same dream" *Ibid.*, p. 43.

Chapter 3

"VERY VERY VERY VERY HORRIBLY NAUGHTY!!!!": Vallone, *Becoming Victoria*, p. 25.

"Two storms – one .... one at washing." Longford, *Queen Victoria*, p. 28.

"There! You see .... *must* about it.": *Ibid.*, p. 31.

"You must not .... call me Victoria.": *Ibid.*, p. 28.

"an upbringing which .... away from her.": Cecil Woodham-Smith, *Queen Victoria: From Her Birth to the Death of the Prince Consort*. (New York: Alfred A. Knopf, 1972), pp. 64-5.

"Above all, the .... extravagant Coburg court...": Hough, *Victoria and Albert*, p. 21.

"different ... of misconduct persisted.": Woodham-Smith, *Queen Victoria*, p. 66.

"give me your little paw": Longford, *Queen Victoria*, p. 27.

"her charming manners.": Grace Greenwood, *Queen Victoria: Her Girlhood and Womanhood*

(Montreal: Dawson Brothers, Publishers, 1883), p. 41.

"The little monkey .... pretty, clever child.": *Ibid.*

"is the most .... her remarkably well.": Woodham-Smith, *Queen Victoria*, p. 70.

"oaths of the .... from an anvil": Greenwood, *Queen Victoria*, p. 44.

"at no time .... or social manners.": John Ashton, *When William IV was King* (London: Chapman & Hall, 1896), p. 6.

"God Save both Queens!": Sandars, *Queen Adelaide*, p. 132.

"My children are .... is mine too.": Greenwood, *Queen Victoria*, p. 45.

"defining the powers .... their legal rights.": Woodham-Smith, *Queen Victoria*, p. 83.

"extremely jealous of .... influence in everything.": Sandars, *Queen Adelaide*, p. 132.

"the Duchess of .... of the King.": Ashton, *When William IV was King*, p. 78.

"Nothing could console .... even my dolls.": Lee, *Queen Victoria*, p. 31.

Chapter 4

"Lilibet walk Self .... love with life.": Asquith, *Her Majesty*, pp. 170-1.

"Why should anybody .... other happy home.": *Ibid.*, p. 167.

"I've got a .... only a bud.": *Ibid.*, p. 173.

"her great-great-grandmother .... and strong opinions.": Erickson, *Lilibet*, p. 20.

"She proved an .... explaining to her.": Marion Crawford, *The Little Princesses* (New York: Harcourt, Brace & World, Inc., 1950), p. 27.

"knew how engrossed .... neighs and winnies." Erickson, *Lilibet*, p. 22.

"the elasticity out .... and thunderous rages": Longford, *The Queen*, p. 53.

"I am beginning .... me for myself.": *Ibid.*, p. 55.

"Lilibet & Margaret looked too sweet.": Pope-Hennessy, *Queen Mary*, p. 556.

"My Darling Lilibet .... polite to everybody.": 29 December 1935, the Duchess of York to Princess Elizabeth, Shawcross, *Counting One's Blessings*, p. 210.

"I pray to God .... and the throne.": Frances Donaldson, *Edward VIII* (Philadelphia: J.B. Lippincott Company, 1974), pp. 185-6.

"After I am dead .... within 12 months.": *Ibid.*, p. 185.

"No reign has .... to his heart.": Bolitho, *George VI*, p. 214.

"Uncle David was …. King were asleep.": Crawford, *Little Princesses*, p. 63.

"he is not responsible to himself alone.": Longford, *The Queen*, p. 61.

"all enthusiasm and …. other American interest [meaning herself].": The Duchess of Windsor, *The Heart Has Its Reasons: The Memoirs of the Duchess of Windsor* (New York: David McKay Company, Inc., 1956), p. 216.

"sitting on the edge of a volcano.": Erickson, *Lilibet*, p. 47.

"This decision has …. save The King.": Duke of Windsor, *A King's Story: The Memoirs of the Duke of Windsor* (New York: G.P. Putnam's Sons), 1947, pp. 411-12.

"Does that mean …. Poor you": Longford, *The Queen*, p. 69.

Chapter 5

"I never saw …. I will be good.": Longford, *Queen Victoria*, p. 32.

"had a soprano …. sweet and true.": Woodham-Smith, *Queen Victoria*, p. 75,

"appears well versed …. and French history.": Vallone, *Becoming Victoria*, p. 67.

"should it be … make others happy.": *Ibid.*

"he urged her .... important and unimportant.": Egon Caesar Conti, *Leopold I of Belgium: Secret Pages of European History*. Translated by John McCabe (London: T. Fisher Unwin Ltd., 1923), p. 92.

"dearest uncle .... like a father": *Ibid.*, p. 94.

"history is the .... *ought* to be.": *Ibid.*, pp. 93-4.

"I never did .... vice and virtue?": Woodham-Smith, *Queen Victoria*, p. 91.

"This Book Mamma .... Wales in it. Victoria.": *Ibid.*, p. 89.

"We close a ... and free country.": Robert Wilson, *The Life and Times of Queen Victoria, Volume I.* (London: Cassell & Company, Ltd., 1891), pp. 15-16.

"I am today .... How *very old*.": Woodham-Smith, *Queen Victoria*, p. 92.

"DEAR SWEET LITTLE DASH": Longford, *Queen Victoria*, p. 46.

"was drowned in .... frightened to death.": Lee, *Queen Victoria*, p. 40.

"I was very .... when we came home.": Longford, *Queen Victoria*, p. 47.

"it seems to .... state of affairs.": Woodham Smith, *Queen Victoria*, pp. 96-7.

"May Your Royal .... *in the future*.": *Ibid.*, p. 98.

Chapter 6

"he had become the prisoner of his heritage.": Windsor, *Heart has Its Reasons*, p. 213.

"his oldest brother …. felt he lacked.": Deborah Cadbury, *Princes at War: The Bitter Battle Inside Britain's Royal Family in the Darkest Days of WW II* (Philadelphia: Public Affairs, 2015), p. 5.

"boyish appearance and … in the family.": Crawford, *Little Princesses*, p. 32.

"by virtue of …. not flatter him.": Cadbury, *Princes at War*, p. 6.

"David's abdication of …. to poor Bertie.": Pope-Hennessy, *Queen Mary*, p. 579.

"With My wife …. lies before Me.": William Shawcross, *The Queen Mother: The Official Biography* (New York: Alfred A. Knopf, 2009), p. 384.

"King George will …. kindliness of heart.": Asquith, *Her Majesty*, p. 216.

"That's *Mummie* now …. suppose it does.": Shawcross, *The Queen Mother*, p. 386.

"in horror …. You mean forever?": Crawford, *Little Princesses*, p. 80.

"used to pray …. to William IV.": Longford, *The Queen*, p. 73.

"It took us …. than a home.": Crawford, *Little Princesses*, p. 87.

"To Mummy and Papa. …. Lilibet by Herself.": Longford, *The Queen*, p. 75.

"nodding with half …. which she passed.": Bolitho, George VI, p. 233.

"an army of …. eight grey horses.": *Ibid.*, p. 234.

"remember that the …. Christ our Redeemer.": *Ibid.*, p. 239.

"The cry of *God* …. over the city.": *Ibid.*, p. 241.

"I thought it …. I thought so.": Erickson, *Lilibet*, pp. 52-3.

"Margaret said, 'I …. I thought charming.": Pope-Hennessy, *Queen Mary*, p. 594.

"My Darling Lilibet …. ever loving Mummy…": 6 May 1939, Queen Elizabeth to Princess Elizabeth, Shawcross, *Counting One's Blessings*, pp. 261-2.

"very beautiful …. Poor old Dookie.": 27 May 1939, Queen Elizabeth to Princess Elizabeth, Shawcross, *Ibid.*, p. 268.

"seemed to me …. irrepressible high spirits…": Ellis, *Thatched with Gold*, p. 225.

"Of the two …. of the two.": Crawford, *Little Princesses*, p. 65.

"Lilibet was far …. expected of her.": *Ibid.*, p. 105.

"I do hope …. not forget that.": 13 May 1939, Queen Elizabeth to Princess Elizabeth, Shawcross, *Counting One's Blessings*, p. 265.

"learnt to love …. make her Queen-Empress.": Longford, *The Queen*, p. 83.

"rather like a …. he can jump.": Crawford, *Little Princesses*, p. 134.

"ignored the awkward …. tendency to dominate.": Erickson, *Lilibet*, p. 62.

Chapter 7

"destined to mount …. of these realms.": September 21st, 1835 entry of Charles Greville in Henry Reeve, ed., *The Greville Memoirs: A Journal of the Reigns of King George IV, King William IV, and Queen Victoria, Volume III*, p. 323.

"He gave me …. dearly for it.": Woodham Smith, *Queen Victoria*, p. 106.

"I can never …. her most dearly …": *Ibid.*, p. 108.

"Those large blue …. into the future.": Longford, *Queen Victoria*, p. 50.

"I resisted in spite of my illness.": *Ibid.*

"Now they are …. can replace them.": Longford, *Queen Victoria*, p. 51.

"I am not fond …. to anything else.": Clarissa Lablache Cheer, *The Great Lablache: Nineteenth Century Operatic Superstar: His Life and Times* (United States: Xlibris, 2009) p. 210.

"immensely powerful …. MOST EXCEEDINGLY DELIGHTED.": *Ibid.*, p. 208.

"There is a tone .... her natural temperament.": *Ibid.*, p. 209.

"self-control diminished .... as Monarch increased.": Sandars, *Queen Adelaide*, p. 257.

"I really cannot .... having brought his.": Woodham Smith, *Queen Victoria*, p. 120.

Chapter 8

"riding their ponies .... room after dinner.": Theo Aronson, *Princess Margaret: A Biography* (Washington, D.C.: Regnery Publishing, Inc., 1997), p. 76.

"who is this Hitler spoiling everything?": Crawford, *Little Princesses*, p. 138.

"stunned": Aronson, *Princess Margaret*, p. 76.

"The children could .... would never go.": Shawcross, *The Queen Mother*, p. 516.

"horrible attack .... tremendous explosion.": 13 September 1940, Queen Elizabeth to Queen Mary, Shawcross, *Counting One's Blessings*, p. 295.

"I'm glad we've .... in the face.": Longford, *The Queen*, p. 95.

"in the end .... to you all.": *Ibid.*

"In that lone .... the hope of Britain.": Erickson, *Lilibet*, p. 74.

"enraged beyond <u>words</u> .... City of London.": 7 January 1941, Queen Elizabeth to Queen Mary, Shawcross, *Counting One's Blessings*, p. 303.

"one of the .... help encouraging her.": Theo Aronson, *Royal Family: Years of Transition* (London: John Murray, 1983), p. 170.

"There was a .... remarked on it.": Crawford, *Little Princesses*, p. 208.

"a simple little service": 10 April 1942, Queen Elizabeth to Queen Mary, Shawcross, *Counting One's Blessings*, p. 320.

"though naturally not .... intelligence and understanding.": Gyles Brandreth, *Philip & Elizabeth: Portrait of a Royal Marriage* (New York: W.W. Norton & Company, 2004), p. 112.

"the carriage of .... Queen Victoria had.": Ellis, *Thatched with Gold*, p. 219.

"had an instinct .... of her character.": Longford, *The Queen*, p. 99.

"extraordinarily handsome .... on our Navy.": Brandreth, *Philip & Elizabeth*, p. 133.

"have been in .... at that age.": Ellis, *Thatched with Gold*, p. 227.

"My eighteenth birthday .... and old friends.": Jane Dismore, *Princess: The Early Life of Queen Elizabeth II* (Lantham, MD: The Rowman & Littlefield Publishing Group, Inc., 2018), p. 181.

"I am glad .... the whole place...": 11 April 1944, Queen Elizabeth to Queen Mary, Shawcross, *Counting One's Blessings*, p. 360.

"She found herself .... and freedom enjoyed.": Ben Pimlott, *The Queen: A Biography of Elizabeth II* (New York: John Wiley & Sons, Inc., 1997), p. 74.

"going to do .... is always useful.": 26 January 1945, Queen Elizabeth to Queen Mary, Shawcross, *Counting One's Blessings*, p. 379.

"trusty squire .... guilty about it.": Lacey, *Monarch*, p. 136.

"unusually lovely nature .... motherly and protective.": Crawford, *Little Princesses*, p. 225.

"unlike her mother .... sparkling younger sister.": Sarah Bradford, *Elizabeth: A Biography of Britain's Queen* (New York: Farrar, Strauss and Giroux, 1996), p. 109.

"was a shy .... social life easy": Bradford, *Elizabeth*, p. 109.

"She was a .... too many problems.": Pimlott, *The Queen*, p. 105.

"Poor darlings, they .... any fun yet.": Aronson, *Royal Family*, p. 169.

Chapter 9

"particularly Albert .... clever and intelligent.": Longford, *Queen Victoria*, p. 52.

"very amiable .... importance to me.": Lee, *Queen Victoria*, p. 44.

"I must thank .... wish to see.": Woodham Smith, *Queen Victoria*, p. 125.

"he neither understood .... disrespectful to him.": Reeve, September 7th, 1836 entry, *Greville Memoirs, Vol. III*, p. 375.

"I trust in God that .... duty to do." September 21st, 1836 entry in *Ibid.*, pp. 375-6.

"she was being .... this critical period.": Woodham Smith, *Queen Victoria*, p.132.

"God knows .... on this fact...": *Ibid.*, p.133.

"Victoria has not written that letter.": Longford, *Queen Victoria*, p. 57.

"you are still .... *talents* and *understanding*.": *Ibid.*, p. 58.

"I could not .... realised in it.": The Duchess of Kent to Lord William Russell, May 8, 1837 in Stockmar, *Memoirs*, p. 375.

"crowds of eager .... the streets impassable.": Ashton, *When William IV was King*, p. 241.

"How old! and .... some day to be!": Woodham Smith, *Queen Victoria*, p.137.

"schemes and intrigues .... the future Sovereign.": Stockmar, *Memoirs*, p. 373.

"the compass": Conti, *Leopold I*, p. 96.

"cool and collected …. apt and determined.": Woodham Smith, *Queen Victoria*, p. 136.

"not at all …. conduct' towards her.": Woodham Smith, *Queen Victoria*, pp. 136.

"if Princess Victoria …. *must be coerced*.": *Ibid.*, p. 140.

"the last barrier between …. was thus removed.": Lee, *Queen Victoria*, p. 48.

"in the gray of the early dawn.": Greenwood, *Queen Victoria*, p. 69.

"very important business …. must give way.": *Ibid.*

"I ask your prayers on my behalf.": John Coulter and John A. Cooper, eds., *Queen Victoria: Her Grand Life and Glorious Reign* (London: C.B. Burrows), p. 22.

"amazed … at her …. but not daunted…": June 21st, 1837 diary entry, Reeve, *Greville Memoirs, Vol. III*, p. 414.

"if she had …. her part better.'" June 21st, 1837 diary entry, *Ibid.*, pp. 414-15.

"self-posession …. I ever saw.": Lee, *Queen Victoria*, p. 50.

"The young Queen …. in her uncle [King William IV].": June 21st, 1837 diary entry, Reeve, *Greville Memoirs, Vol. III*, p. 418.

Chapter 10

"beside some well-loved …. out of sight": Queen Alexandra of Yugoslavia, *Prince Philip: A Family Portrait* (Indianapolis: The Bobbs-Merrill Company, Inc., 1959), p. 102.

"The briskness of …. son-in-law slightly unappealing.": Philip Eade, *Prince Philip: The Turbulent Early Life of the Man Who Married Queen Elizabeth II* (New York: Henry Holt and Company, 2011), p. 181.

"it was simply …. long as possible.": Aronson, *Royal Family*, p. 170.

"There was no …. a fortune-hunter.": Pimlott, *The Queen*, p. 105.

"the self-reliance bred …. to fawning deference.": Eade, *Prince Philip*, pp. 180-1.

"I declare before …. share in it.": Aronson, *Royal Family*, p. 172.

"lived though some …. and wise understanding.": Dismore, *Princess*, pp. 214-15.

"As it was …. was with Philip.": Brandreth, *Philip & Elizabeth*, p. 134.

"how happy we …. beloved little daughter.": 9 July 1947, Queen Elizabeth to Prince Philip (Lieutenant Philip Mountbatten, R.N.), Shawcross, *Counting One's Blessings*, p. 401.

"Heard with great .... luncheon looking radiant.":
Pope-Hennessy, *Queen Mary*, p. 615.

"Observing him I .... helped Queen Victoria.":
Ellis, *Thatched with Gold*, pp. 228-9.

"When I looked .... air of majesty.": *Ibid*., p. 228.

"in grey, war-wracked .... in the world."
Aronson, *Royal Family*, p. 177.

"victorious Britain seemed .... on her knees.":
Shawcross, *The Queen Mother*, p. 627.

"I can't believe .... keep pinching myself.":
Crawford, *Little Princesses*, p. 280.

"one wanted to .... at the heart.": Queen
Alexandra, *Prince Philip*, p. 117.

"I was so .... in our work.": Bradford, *Elizabeth*,
pp. 131-2.

"Darling Lilibet, no .... my one wish ...": 24
November 1947, Queen Elizabeth to Princess
Elizabeth, Shawcross, *Counting One's Blessings*, p.
402.

"Lilibet is the .... and for us.": Shawcross, *The
Queen Mother*, p. 631.

"the baby is .... happy for them.": 5 January 1949,
Queen Elizabeth to Prince Paul of Yugoslavia,
Shawcross, *Counting One's Blessings*, p. 413.

"look out for yourselves.": Queen Alexandra,
Prince Philip, p. 162.

"he did not .... only a child.": Shawcross, *The Queen Mother*, p. 654.

"It is hard .... such a burden.": 6 February 1952, Queen Elizabeth to Queen Mary, Shawcross, *Countng One's Blessings*, p. 444.

"weeping desperately for .... straightened up": Erickson, *Lilibet*, p. 127.

"My own name .... 'Elizabeth.'": Brandreth, *Philip & Elizabeth*, p. 213.

"Oh, I'm so .... home, I'm afraid.": Erickson, *Lilibet*, p. 127.

"the end of .... life had come.": *Ibid.*, p. 129.

"Her old Grannie .... the British Crown.": Pope-Hennessy, *Queen Mary*, p. 620.

"I commend to .... has been called.": 18 February 1952, Queen Elizabeth's message to the nation, Shawcross, *Counting One's Blessings*, p. 447.

BIBLIOGRAPHY

Queen Victoria:

Ashton, John. *When William IV was King*. London: Chapman & Hall, 1896.

Cheer, Clarissa Lablache. *The Great Lablache: Nineteenth Century Operatic Superstar: His Life and Times*. United States: Xlibris, 2009.

Conti, Egon Caesar. *Leopold I of Belgium: Secret Pages of European History*. Translated by John McCabe. London: T. Fisher Unwin Ltd., 1923.

Coulter, John and John A. Cooper, eds., *Queen Victoria: Her Grand Life and Glorious Reign*. London: C.B. Burrows, 1901.

Greenwood, Grace. *Queen Victoria: Her Girlhood and Womanhood*. Montreal: Dawson Brothers, 1883.

Hough, Richard. *Victoria and Albert*. New York: St. Martin's Press, 1996.

Lee, Sidney. *Queen Victoria: A Biography*. London: John Murray, 1904.

Longford, Elizabeth. *Queen Victoria: Born to Succeed*. New York: Harper & Row, Publishers, 1964.

Reeve, Henry, ed., *The Greville Memoirs: A Journal of the Reigns of King George IV, King William IV, and Queen Victoria, Volume III*. London: Longmans, Green, and Co., 1905.

Sandars, Mary F. *The Life and Times of Queen Adelaide*. London: Stanley Paul & Co., 1915.

Stockmar, Baron E. von. *Memoirs of Baron Stockmar*. Edited by F. Max Müller. London: Longmans, Green, and Co., 1873.

Vallone, Lynn. *Becoming Victoria*. New Haven, CT: Yale University Press, 2001.

Wilson, Robert. *The Life and Times of Queen Victoria, Volume I*. London: Cassell & Company, Ltd., 1900.

Woodham-Smith, Cecil. *Queen Victoria: From Her Birth to the Death of the Prince Consort*. New York: Alfred A. Knopf, 1972.

Queen Elizabeth II:

Queen Alexandra of Yugoslavia, *Prince Philip: A Family Portrait*. Indianapolis: The Bobbs-Merrill Company, Inc., 1959.

Aronson, Theo. *Princess Margaret: A Biography*. Washington, D.C.: Regnery Publishing, Inc., 1997.

------------------. *Royal Family: Years of Transition*. London: John Murray, 1983.

Asquith, Lady Cynthia. *Her Majesty the Queen: An Entirely New and Complete Biography*. New York: E.P. Dutton & Company, 1937.

Bolitho, Hector. *King George VI*. Philadelphia: J.B. Lippincott Company, 1938.

Bradford, Sarah. *Elizabeth: A Biography of Britain's Queen*. New York: Farrar, Strauss and Giroux, 1996.

Brandreth, Gyles. *Philip & Elizabeth: Portrait of a Royal Marriage*. New York: W.W. Norton & Company, 2004.

Cadbury, Deborah. *Princes at War: The Bitter Battle Inside Britain's Royal Family in the Darkest Days of WW II*. Philadelphia: Public Affairs, 2015.

Crawford, Marion. *The Little Princesses*. New York: Harcourt, Brace & World, Inc., 1950.

Dismore, Jane. *Princess: The Early Life of Queen Elizabeth II*. Lantham, MD: The Rowman & Littlefield Publishing Group, Inc., 2018.

Donaldson, Frances. *Edward VIII*. Philadelphia: J.B. Lippincott Company, 1974.

Eade, Philip. *Prince Philip: The Turbulent Early Life of the Man Who Married Queen Elizabeth II*. New York: Henry Holt and Company, 2011.

Ellis, Jennifer, ed., *Thatched with Gold: The Memoirs of Mabell, Countess of Airlie*. London: Hutchinson of London, 1962.

Erickson, Carolly. *Lilibet: An Intimate Portrait of Elizabeth II*. New York: St. Martin's Press, 2004.

Lacey, Robert. *Monarch: The Life and Reign of Elizabeth II*. New York: Free Press, 2002.

Longford, Elizabeth. *The Queen: The Life of Elizabeth II*. New York: Alfred A. Knopf, 1983.

------------------------. *Elizabeth R: A Biography*. London: Hodder & Stoughton, 1984.

Pimlott, Ben. *The Queen: A Biography of Elizabeth II*. New York: John Wiley & Sons, 1997.

Pope-Hennessy, James. *Queen Mary, 1867-1953*. London: George Allen and Unwin, Ltd., 1959.

Shawcross, William, ed., *Counting One's Blessings: The Selected Letters of Queen Elizabeth the Queen Mother*. New York: Farrar, Straus and Giroux, 2012.

-----------------------. *The Queen Mother: The Official Biography*. New York: Alfred A. Knopf, 2009.

Windsor, Duchess of. *The Heart Has Its Reasons: The Memoirs of the Duchess of Windsor*. New York: David McKay Company, Inc., 1956.

Windsor, Duke of. *A King's Story: The Memoirs of the Duke of Windsor*. New York: G.P. Putnam's Sons, 1947.

FURTHER READING

Books on Queen Victoria and Queen Elizabeth II are plentiful and those who wish to read further on both queens are spoilt for choice. The following are some of the works that are well worth one's time reading.

Queen Victoria

Arnstein, Walter L. *Queen Victoria*. New York: Palgrave Macmillan, 2003.

Hibbert, Christopher. *Queen Victoria in Her Letters and Journals*. Stroud, UK: Sutton Publishing, 2000.

Longford, Elizabeth. *Queen Victoria: Born to Succeed*. New York: Harper & Row, Publishers, 1964.

Weintraub, Stanley. *Queen Victoria: An Intimate Biography*.

Woodham-Smith, Cecil. *Queen Victoria: From Her Birth to the Death of the Prince Consort*. New York: Alfred A. Knopf, 1972.

<u>Queen Elizabeth II</u>

Bradford, Sarah. *Elizabeth: A Biography of Britain's Queen*. New York: Farrar, Strauss and Giroux, 1996.

Erickson, Carolly. *Lilibet: An Intimate Portrait of Elizabeth II*. New York: St. Martin's Press, 2004.

Longford, Elizabeth. *The Queen: The Life of Elizabeth II*. New York: Alfred A. Knopf, 1983.

Pimlott, Ben. *The Queen: A Biography of Elizabeth II*. New York: John Wiley & Sons, 1997.

.

ABOUT THE AUTHOR

Julia P. Gelardi is an independent historian. After obtaining a Master of Arts degree in history from Simon Fraser University in Canada, Julia has written books and articles focusing on European royalty. She currently resides in Minnesota with her husband.

BOOKS BY THE AUTHOR

Born to Rule: Five Reigning Consorts, Granddaughters of Queen Victoria (2005)

In Triumph's Wake: Royal Mothers, Tragic Daughters, and the Price They Paid for Glory (2009)

From Splendor to Revolution: The Romanov Women, 1847-1928 (2011)

A Guarded Secret: Tsar Nicholas II, Tsarina Alexandria and Tsarevich Alexei's Hemophilia (2018)

Made in the USA
Columbia, SC
24 December 2019

85741834R10093